PREVENTION THAT WORKS!

SAFETY & SECURITY

This book is lovingly dedicated to my husband,
Timothy Knowles.

PREVENTION THAT WORKS!

A Guide for Developing School-Based
Drug and Violence Prevention Programs

CYNTHIA R. KNOWLES

CORWIN PRESS, INC.
A Sage Publications Company
Thousand Oaks, California

For information:

Corwin Press, Inc.
A Sage Publications Company
2455 Teller Road
Thousand Oaks, California 91320
E-mail: order@corwinpress.com

Sage Publications Ltd.
6 Bonhill Street
London EC2A 4PU
United Kingdom

Sage Publications India Pvt. Ltd.
M-32 Market
Greater Kailash I
New Delhi 110 048 India

Printed in the United States of America

Library of Congress Cataloging-in-Publication Data

Knowles, Cynthia R.
    Prevention that works! A guide for developing school-based drug and violence prevention programs / by Cynthia R. Knowles.
        p.   cm.
    Includes bibliographical references and index.
    ISBN 0-7619-7804-6 (c: alk. paper) — ISBN 0-7619-7805-4 (p: alk. paper)
    1. School violence—United States—Prevention—Evaluation.   2. Students—Drug use—United States—Prevention—Evaluation.   I. Title.
    LB3013.3 .K55 2001
    371.7′8′0973—dc21   2001000298

This book is printed on acid-free paper.

01   02   03   04   05   06   07   7   6   5   4   3   2   1

Acquiring Editor:	Robb Clouse
Corwin Editorial Assistant:	Kylee Liegl
Production Editor:	Diane S. Foster
Editorial Assistant:	Kathryn Journey
Typesetter/Designer:	Lynn Miyata
Indexer:	Cristina Haley
Cover Designer:	Michelle Lee

Contents

Preface

The recent publicity surrounding schoolyard shootings resulted in nothing less than a frenzied reaction by schools around the country as they scrambled to implement violence prevention programs to protect their students. These violence prevention programs were developed quickly, often with little empirical information on proven methods, effective program content, or design. Even worse, in most cases these programs, and often hefty expenditures, were based on a need that had been assumed as a result of media hype, not a need that had been proved through the examination of local data (U.S. Department of Education & U.S. Department of Justice, 1999).

The field of violence prevention is still in its infancy. Even though more than 80 violence prevention programs are currently being marketed, few of them have undergone evaluation studies of their outcome effectiveness. Only a dozen of them have been evaluated in the scientific literature, but none have been adequately measured postprogram (for at least 2 years) to show effectiveness in changing student attitudes or behaviors. That puts the burden of proving effectiveness back on the school or agency that uses these programs (Drug Strategies, 1998).

During the last 30 or so years, substance abuse prevention has been through this same process of responding to crisis, failing to be effective, being assessed and reassembled more thoughtfully, and finally being successful. We can learn by examining drug prevention efforts and not make the same mistakes a second time in this new arena of violence prevention.

The primary source of funding for school-based drug and violence prevention programs has been the federal Safe and Drug Free Schools and Communities program (Title IV), a part of the U.S. Department of Education. Since 1986, all schools, public and private, have received this entitlement money. This is one of those wonderful programs that, following an application to the state education department, sends money directly to local districts to be used for prevention efforts they select themselves, based on their individual needs.

As is often the case with programs this large, accountability at the local level has been lacking. Despite the growing availability of information on effective programs, schools continue to use programs that have not been proven effective. Some are using model programs but have changed the content or design enough so that the features that once made the programs effective are gone. Or worse, they are using programs that have been proven *ineffective* simply because that is what is easiest or most familiar (Bangert-Downs, 1988).

In 1998, the U.S. Department of Education, in an effort to improve accountability, move schools away from ineffective prevention, and increase the use of "proven" programs, issued a list of Safe and Drug Free Schools Principles of Effectiveness (U.S. Department of Education, 1998b) (see Resource A). The Principles of Effectiveness outline a process for using data to reassess violence and substance abuse prevention needs, select effective programs based on measurable objectives, and evaluate the resulting programs for effectiveness in meeting those objectives.

To underscore the necessity of determining program effectiveness, consider the results of a recent survey of drug education programs conducted by the University of North Carolina at Chapel Hill's School of Public Health (and funded by the Robert Wood Johnson Foundation). Lead researcher Dr. Hallfors found that 82% of schools are still using the DARE program despite repeated studies showing that DARE is ineffective in reducing later substance use behaviors. Even with a growing body of research identifying prevention programs that are effective, DARE remains the most widely used program among schools studied. In fact, the three most widely used programs—DARE, Hear's Looking at You, and McGruff's Drug Prevention and Child Protection—have little to no peer-reviewed research to show that they are effective in preventing drug use and other risk behaviors. Dr. Hallfors found that a significant number of the schools involved in her survey were not familiar with the Principles of Effectiveness. Of the schools familiar with these principles, only 14% said they had developed an evaluation plan for their current program.

In November 2000, the Rand Corporation conducted a similar review of delinquency prevention programs (Rand Corporation Drug Policy Research Center, http://www.rand.org/centers/dprc). Peter Greenwood, a crime-prevention expert, found that funders tend to support programs that are high profile and eye-catching, but ineffective. His recommendation was quite simple: *Read.* Read the growing body of research and select prevention programs that we know work.

But even when schools implemented "proven" curricula, there were problems. Of all the schools in the Chapel Hill study that had selected the Reconnecting Youth program, a program with proven effectiveness, only one was using it as prescribed. All the other schools had made adaptations and changes to the delivery model despite the lack of research supporting the effectiveness of such changes.

It has been suggested that these ineffective programs continue because they are easy, low-to-no-cost, and often require no teacher training or commitment from the district. In contrast, adhering to the Principles of Effectiveness or assessing a program requires tremendous commitment, sometimes rigorous teacher training, substantial budgeting of time and money, and ongoing measurement and data collection.

This task is particularly overwhelming because you and I both know who will end up doing all that work. The job of developing and implementing effective prevention programs will fall to the District Health Coordinator, the Prevention Specialist, the Drug Counselor, or the Student Assistance Professional—a person with little to no training in research methods and no spare time.

This book is written for you, the guy or gal in the trenches. Use this as a guide, a reference. Each chapter should stand on its own so that it will meet you where you are in the process. Mark the pages, copy the worksheets. Follow the process that's outlined here from beginning to end, and not only will you have an effective prevention program, but you'll be able to prove it. I've even included tips for preparing your results for public presentations, for the media, and for securing additional money.

We can no longer afford to implement ineffective programs. Even if the Principles of Effectiveness do not apply to you, your programming, or your funding, it's still a good idea to establish careful outcome measures that show your program was effective in changing student behavior. Use this guide if you are a student, program staff, board member, police officer, or parent who needs to know whether a program is making a difference. If you are new to the process of measuring program effectiveness, this guide will walk you fearlessly from start to finish.

I hope this book is a help to you as you create and implement programs to meet the needs of your students and prepare them for safe and healthy lives.

Acknowledgments

With sincere gratitude I acknowledge the following people for their help, both professional and personal, in my efforts to complete this book:

My mother, Margaret Nichols, and father, Maurice Mutimer, were both scientists. Thanks, Mom and Dad, for teaching me to think in a logical way.

My thanks to childhood friend and now adult lawyer friend, David O'Connell, who keeps me laughing and safe from legal harm.

Thanks to Michael Doughty, a good friend and a really, really smart man, who went through these pages sentence by sentence, teaching me more than a thing or two about proper grammar.

I'd like to thank the employees at the U.S. Department of Education for being very nongovernmental in answering all my questions promptly and accurately via telephone and e-mail.

Thanks to Robb Clouse, my editor at Corwin Press, who liked what he read and walked me through this entire process from start to finish.

I especially would like to thank all the schools that have welcomed me in to work with them over the years. I have learned the most in my professional life sitting around those tables, sifting through piles of data and survey results, eating pizza, listening to stories, and swapping anecdotes. Those rooms, and time with such dedicated people, have been my real education about program development.

Thank you to the scores of students who have participated on committees with me, been in focus groups, done presentations and trainings with me, and have shown me what I wasn't seeing. From where I sit, our future looks like it's in very capable hands.

Thanks also to the following reviewers: Barbara J. Ettner, Policy Analyst, Virginia Board for People With Disabilities, Richmond, Virginia; Professor Abbot L. Packard, Northern Iowa University, Cedar Falls; James R. Sanders, The Evaluation Center, Western Michigan University, Kalamazoo; and Phillip S. Abode, Office of Research, Evaluation, and Assessment, Fresno (California) Unified School District.

To my husband, thank you for the quiet days and every other single thing.

—Cynthia R. Knowles

About the Author

Cynthia R. Knowles works nationally helping schools, agencies, and businesses maximize the effectiveness of their prevention programs through student and employee training, curriculum review, data analysis, awareness education, and program evaluation. She works as the Health and Wellness Coordinator at Livonia Central School, Livonia, New York; as a lecturer at the State University of New York at Geneseo; as a supervisor of student teachers in health education at the State University of New York at Cortland; and as a professional ski instructor.

Previously she has been the Director of Rehabilitation for a 135-bed homeless shelter, a psychotherapist for adolescents and their families, and a regional coordinator for the Safe and Drug Free Schools grant program. Through articles and training seminars, she advocates for truth, accuracy, and youth involvement in the field of violence and substance abuse. She teaches participants to question their sources and to validate all information before passing it on.

Her politics are simple: She believes that all of us—parents, teachers, and neighbors—have the ability to change the world significantly through our interactions with youth. She believes in prayer and miracles but is still slightly superstitious and overinsured.

Cynthia welcomes your feedback, especially your experiences, challenges, insights, and successes with using this book for program evaluation. You may contact Mrs. Knowles at *cknowles@localnet.com*. She lives in rural western New York with her husband and son.

Getting Started

Establishing Your Work Group

Truth is stranger than fiction, and often it's a lot harder to believe.

—Unknown

"I'm not a scientist! I just want to help people. That's what I went to school for, and that's what I'm good at." This is the cry of today's prevention worker. Until a few years ago, a prevention specialist didn't have to know much about program development, program assessment, or outcome measures. All we had to do was pull the puppet out of the box and read the script that came with it to a classroom full of children. A few years later, when some of those same children began using drugs, we were discouraged. "Why didn't it work?" "What else could we have done?"

Those two questions are the basis for program development and program assessment. You are probably reading this book because one or both of those tasks have recently been added to your job description. Developing an effective program and assessing program effectiveness has become your responsibility because you (a) have received competitive state or federal funds to implement new programs, (b) coordinate the Safe and Drug Free Schools program, (c) are trying to market your program to a school district that needs to see proof of effectiveness, or (d) simply want to know whether what you have been doing all these years is effective at preventing drug use and violence in the youth you serve.

In 1998, the U.S. Department of Education announced that all funds received under Title IV—Safe and Drug Free Schools and Communities Act State Grant programs—would be governed by the Principles of Effectiveness

(U.S. Department of Education, 1998b) (see Resource A). Most school-based programs that are designed to reduce violence and substance abuse are funded with this money. Once people really understood the Principles, a wave of fear moved though the prevention community. Adhering to the Principles would require data collection, program adjustments, and (gasp!) mathematics. Not only would this become one more responsibility of the already overextended prevention worker, but this also meant that some programs—and jobs—might be eliminated because of the absence of proper "proof" of effectiveness. Suddenly, we all have to show that what we do is effective at changing student behavior.

The Principles of Effectiveness were developed after numerous studies showed that state and federal prevention funding was sometimes misused or spent on eye-catching programs that were aggressively marketed but often not evaluated for their effectiveness in changing drug use and violent behaviors (Dryfoos, 1993; Klitzner, 1987; Sherman et al., 1997). Safe and Drug Free Schools funds were even being spent on programs that had been shown to be ineffective. An exhaustive review of program availability, selection, and implementation funded by the federal government in 1996 (Sherman et al., 1997) showed that research had determined what effective **prevention** methods and techniques were, but most prevention programs still used what was easy or familiar rather than what actually worked (Sherman et al., 1987). The Principles of Effectiveness were developed to start prevention program providers thinking in terms of effectiveness.

These Principles of Effectiveness may or may not apply to you directly, but they do provide a logical and well-grounded direction for how to develop and assess effective programming.

▶ The Principles of Effectiveness

Principle 1

The first principle states that all program implementation will be based on **objective data** about drug use and violence specific to the school and community being served. This means that if you want to continue with a violence prevention program already in place, then you will have to produce the *data,* or the actual numbers, proving that a violence problem that needs preventing exists in the first place.

This principle makes good sense because collecting data and measuring first makes good sense. You would never think about buying curtains for a window you had not measured. You could probably make a good guess, but the curtains wouldn't fit their best unless you measured first. Similarly, you can't fit a program to your population unless you measure that population's needs first. Many communities that have resisted data collection efforts and student surveys will now have to do these things to ensure effective programming and continued funding.

Principle 2

The second principle states that programming will be developed with measurable program goals and objectives based on the data collected and will rely on "proven" programs to meet those goals and objectives. This programming is to be developed with the assistance of a local or regional advisory council. Principle 1 helped us collect the data to determine the actual needs of our population; now Principle 2 directs us to develop programming based on those actual needs. It also specifies that an advisory council representing the school-community be involved. This process is intended to do the following:

▶ Eliminate the continuation of ineffective programs.

▶ Eliminate decisions being made by a single person.

▶ Eliminate continued use of programs that are not meeting the actual needs of your population.

▶ Support changes in program direction or program content.

Principle 3

The third principle directs us to select program designs and activities based on scientific research that provides evidence that the strategies used actually reduce or prevent drug use or violence. There is a rich, extensive collection of research on what really works to reduce student drug use and to change attitudes and behaviors. This includes direction on selecting packaged programs, teaching techniques, classroom management, school organizational strategies, and leadership styles, all of which have been proven to reduce substance use and violence. Principle 3 ensures the following:

▶ Schools involved in ineffective practices will now be encouraged to replace them with proven approaches.

▶ Safe and Drug Free Schools and other state and federal money previously spent on T-shirts, pencils, and narrowly focused, short-term programs will now be better spent on more effective strategies.

▶ Lists and collections of "proven and promising programs" will be distributed from a variety of sources to simplify the program selection process.

▶ We will all become much more informed consumers of prevention programming.

Principle 3 also means, however, that all Safe and Drug Free Schools or similarly funded programming currently in place must either be replaced with "proven" programs or "proven" methods or be evaluated to prove that they are themselves effective programs. This second option is the area that seems to strike a chord of concern with prevention workers.

Countless homegrown programs are out there, and many have never been formally measured for their outcome effectiveness. These homegrown programs have been written and designed, not by scientists, but by school counselors, social workers, therapists, agency staff, teachers and students, or just about anyone else who works with youth. Some of these are creative, accurately targeted, and well-implemented programs, but they just haven't been evaluated. Now they will have to be if certain state and federal funding is to continue to support them.

Principle 4

The fourth principle states that programs will be periodically evaluated to assess progress toward achieving goals and objectives (see Resource B, "Resources for Evaluation"). It initially sounds as if all that's needed to meet this principle is a sound data collection system. Principle 4 goes on to state, however, that programs that are unable to demonstrate positive outcomes in reducing drug use or violence must be discontinued.

What does all this mean to you? It means that, like it or not, the federal government is going to pull you either willingly or kicking and screaming into the world of science. Say good-bye to easy answers, assessment by opinion, doing what you've always done, and blissful ignorance of statistics. Welcome instead to the valid and reliable world of controlled experiments, separation of variables, and number crunching!

◤ Where to Begin

You have to begin developing new programs and protecting your old prevention programs with a structured plan that will measure your program's outcomes. You will need to collect, organize, and present irrefutable evidence supporting the effectiveness of the work you are doing. This is a necessary process and will help you do the following:

▶ Develop an organized data collection system so that you'll know exactly the needs of your population.

▶ Develop programming that is uncluttered, streamlined, and less hit-and-miss because it will be based on the actual needs of your population.

▶ Discontinue ineffective program practices.

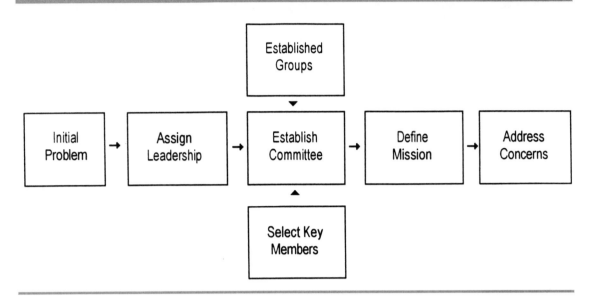

♠ FIGURE 1.1. Program Development: Flowchart 1

▶ Establish a system for program assessment that will ensure accurate information for refining, improving, and strengthening your prevention program.

▶ Provide accurate feedback to program planners.

▶ Provide real accountability, through your quantitative data, to program supporters and funders.

▶ Have real data and "proof" to report program progress and success.

The following five steps will provide an organized beginning to the process of developing effective programs (see Figure 1.1).

Identify the Problem

The first step in developing an effective program is to identify the general problem the program is supposed to fix. This often happens naturally as a concern or question that comes from an administrator, teacher, school staff, or students. "We have to do something about the smoking in the bathrooms." "The last survey we gave students showed that we had an increase in drug use among ninth graders." "Do we need to look at some character education programs?" "I'm concerned about the youth violence I'm hearing about on TV. Maybe we should get a violence prevention program here." Identify the problem and write it down.

Assign Leadership

Once the problem has been identified, someone needs to be in charge. The second step, therefore, is assigning leadership. When selecting a project leader, keep in mind that this process will take time and require a knowledgeable leader who is very organized and who is respected by the school community. Try to avoid giving this assignment to someone who is already overloaded with responsibilities. It simply won't get done. Some districts create a part-time position or expand a current employee to full-time. Using volunteers as committee members is fine, but leadership needs to be a paid position.

Form a Work Group

No one person should be responsible for developing and assessing a program. This is definitely a team effort, working best if a committee or group is in place to help with the data collection, data review, and interpretation. Thus the third step is forming a work group. When determining who should be involved, consider the purpose of your project. If you are developing a drug or violence prevention program, then you will probably want on your committee those individuals who are involved with prevention or health education. If you are assessing implementation or teaching techniques, then you will want more teachers involved. Ideally, this process of data collection and program development will dovetail with the work of preexisting groups, committees, and advisory councils.

Make a real effort to access these preexisting groups, committees, and advisory councils. Most districts have a building planning team, a school improvement team, a health advisory committee, and a Safe and Drug Free Schools advisory group. These groups may already be involved with data collection and the development and assessment of programs. Each of these groups needs similar data in order to do their work. It makes sense to work in cooperation with each other to avoid duplication of efforts.

Because effective violence and drug prevention programming will overlap between these groups, it's a good idea to have broad-based representation from all of them. By creating a blended group that represents a cross section of your community and school programs, you will have a head start in building support for your programs. Starting with the cooperative endeavor of data collection will also assist all groups in working together to implement the most effective and comprehensive programs.

Key members for your group may include the following:

▶ *A district employee* who fully understands the software used to track all student referrals.

▶ *Classroom teachers* at the grade level where you will be implementing programs.

> This group has been assembled by [authority],
> with the support of the Board of Education,
> to assess the effectiveness of [district] drug and
> violence prevention programs in a manner
> that involves all stakeholders and results in
> recommended changes that will increase the
> effectiveness of current programming.

▶ *Parents and students* who will be participating in the programs that are being assessed.

▶ *Members of other key groups and committees* in your school-community, including local businesses and service agencies.

▶ *People with expertise or interest in drug and violence prevention programming.*

▶ *School board members and an administrator;* it's nice to have representation and support from the real decision makers.

▶ *Members from your anticipated opposition;* having this group involved from the very start will reduce program opposition and increase favorable word-of-mouth around the community.

Make sure the people who have committed to help with data collection/ analysis and program development and assessment have the time to do this job in a thorough and accurate manner. In some cases, Title IV money can be used to pay stipends for this type of committee work.

Define the Mission

Once this group is together, they need to define their purpose. Thus the fourth step is defining the mission. Refer back to the initially identified "problem" that began this process. What concern brought this group together in the first place? Did an event or incident lead to this assignment? What is the purpose for developing this program? Who's in charge? Is there administrative support? Is there a timeline for finishing this job? As a group, write a mission statement (see Figure 1.2 for a sample).

Address Concerns at the Beginning

Do we really have to do all this? How do we narrow our focus? It's difficult to sift through everything to determine what is relevant and necessary. This looks very expensive, confusing, and time intensive. How often will this group have to meet? Will we get release-time or stipends? Do we have access to any money? Do we even have a place to meet? This will take *how* long? It seems easier just to do nothing and take our chances.

You do not have to conduct an assessment of all your programming in the first year. To be thorough, you will want to look at consistency of implementation, collect some outcome data to make sure your program is doing what you say it is doing, and monitor your time/cost effectiveness to make things easier when you repeat the program. That's all there is to the fifth step, addressing concerns at the beginning.

With a little planning, you can estimate costs for your work group activities up front and work it into your budget. Program development and assessment need not be confusing, time-consuming, or expensive. This book will walk you through a systematic process of data review, establishment of goals and objectives, collection and synthesis of assessment data, and adjustment of your program to maximize effectiveness. This will be done in normal language, with the only assumption being that you have never done it before.

▣ Conclusion

At the 12th Annual National Prevention Network Research Conference in Buffalo, New York (October 1999), General Barry McCaffrey, Director of the Office of National Drug Control Policy—Office of the President, defended plans to shift Safe and Drug Free Schools money from entitlement to competitive funds. He said that this proposed change in funding was attributable to an "absence of measurable results" and that future funding increases to the Safe and Drug Free Schools program would not occur until there was more accountability for program effectiveness.

Another motivation for developing more effective programs is money. The better able you are to prove that what you are doing is working, the more money will be available to you. The more money at your disposal, the more staff training and programming you can do. The result will be healthier and safer students, and that is everyone's ultimate goal.

Second Thoughts ◀

▶ The Principles of Effectiveness were designed to help prevention program providers think in terms of "What's going to be most effective?" rather than "What's the easiest way to do this?"

▶ Structured program development will enhance your program's implementation, effectiveness, and accountability.

▶ Program development efforts can be time-consuming and require a credible, knowledgeable, paid leader.

▶ Program development is a team effort, requiring a committed group of people with a genuine interest in ensuring effective programs.

▶ Organization, role definition, and a clear mission will streamline the process and ensure greater effectiveness.

2 Writing Goals and Objectives

It is wrong always, everywhere, and for anyone, to believe anything upon insufficient data.

—William Kingdon Clifford

To develop an effective program, it is necessary to explore why it is being created in the first place. What is this program expected to do? How will participants look once they've completed this program? Not only will the establishment of goals and objectives help focus the development of your program, but the objectives will provide a timeline as well as a basis for later assessment of program effectiveness.

Before writing program goals and objectives, the work group needs to be clear on exactly what they are doing. Which grade levels will be the focus of the program? What behaviors or attitudes will be changed in participants? Will implementation be broad or narrow? Will staff training be necessary? How much will this cost?

This chapter walks you through the following four steps (see Figure 2.1).

▶ Identifying Data Sources

Begin at the End

To write or rewrite realistic goals and objectives, it is necessary to start at the end. Ask yourself, "What will these students look like after they receive this program?" Will they be less likely to engage in violent behaviors? Will they engage in lower rates of tobacco use? Will they show a delayed onset of alcohol use? Exactly what are you trying to accomplish with this program? (If you are unable to articulate clearly what you hope to accomplish with an

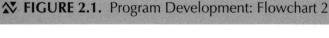

FIGURE 2.1. Program Development: Flowchart 2

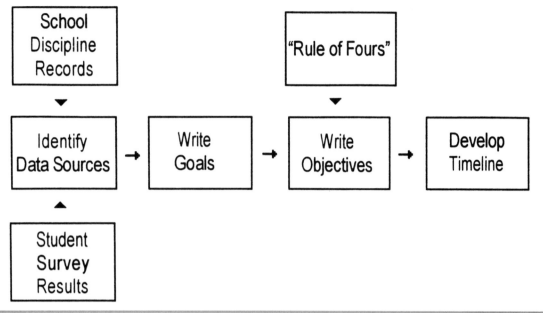

existing program, then you may want to look more closely at the viability of continuing that program or activity.) Once you can name exactly what behavior you would like to see changed as a result of successful programming, start looking for data that measure rates of that specific behavior.

Look at the initial data your work group has collected. These may include the results of a recent survey or your school's discipline data. Look for patterns, and identify a population or age-group that stands out as displaying behaviors of higher risk. Identify the specific problem behaviors you would like to see changed. (Additional sources of data are reviewed in Chapter 5.)

Real Versus Perceived Needs

Be careful when identifying needs to differentiate between *real needs* and *perceived needs*. The area of violence and substance abuse prevention can be a very emotional one. People quite often make unsubstantiated statements of need with great passion and conviction.

"What these students really need is to increase their self-esteem; that would solve a lot of problems." In fact, unless you have specifically measured your students' self-esteem levels and can determine through comparison with baseline, state, or national data that the self-esteem of your students is either low or dropping, then this statement about self-esteem is based on perceived need rather than on real need. Significant research also indicates that our students are not suffering from low self-esteem and that programs designed to raise self-esteem are not effective in changing drug use or violent behaviors.

"My son tells me that everyone is smoking marijuana; he can't go anywhere without having it offered to him. He even sees it in school." Again, this statement is based on a perceived need, not on a real analysis of the data. If you have student survey results, then you will probably find that not "everyone" is smoking marijuana. Refer back to the objective data; they will support or disprove perceived need statements like this one.

"We have to do something about all the violence; our children aren't safe in schools anymore. We need metal detectors and video cameras." This perceived need is very common. Again, check your objective data. Is the incidence of violent crime among 12- to 18-year-olds increasing in your community? How about school data on weapon confiscation and fighting? Is escalating violence really a problem in your community? Don't let the media cloud your thinking on issues of drugs and violence. Not all communities are like the ones on television. Always refer back to your objective data.

Other sources of perceived needs include the following:

- ▶ Opinion surveys
- ▶ Anecdotal information
- ▶ Feedback from staff, students, parents
- ▶ Focus group information
- ▶ Some press/media reports
- ▶ Meeting minutes/group discussions
- ▶ Poorly collected data (e.g., small sample size, skewed population sample)

These information sources are all important; they just aren't objective. If you run student focus groups (see Chapter 6) and learn that students perceive a high level of marijuana use, then it is important to collect more objective data to prove or disprove this perception. If perceived needs are not validated or proved by objective data, then you know to begin education and awareness programming to correct the misperceptions. The perceived need is where data collection and programming ideas *start*. The objective data are used to ensure that programs are properly targeted in terms of content and age-group.

Once specific problems have been identified with your objective data, it's time to write your program goals and objectives.

▣ Writing Goals

For some people, writing goals and objectives can be an overwhelming task. The pressure to do it "right" or to do it by a particular set of standards sometimes makes us overthink exactly what we are doing. That can lead to some poorly written and confusing goal statements.

A **goal** is a statement of direction and intent. *Merriam-Webster's Collegiate Dictionary* defines a goal as "the end toward which effort is directed" (1998, p. 499). Below are some examples of program goals. As you can see, they are broad, general, umbrella statements.

► Institute a peer mediation program.

► Hire a middle school counselor.

► Collect baseline data.

► Reduce campus smoking.

You will generally only have a few goals for your program each year.

Suppose your grandmother asks you to tell her three things you hope to accomplish this year at school. You would keep your answer largely nontechnical and say, "I'm going to start a mentoring program, refine our elementary prevention curriculum, and focus on decreasing smoking on campus." Congratulations, you have just written your prevention goals for this year! A goal is a simple statement of one sentence that describes the direction or end result of your programming efforts.

Now what will you say when Grandma then asks, "How do you know that's what needs to be done?" If you tell her, "It's just common sense," or, "This is what's being done in drug and violence prevention now," or, "This is what I was told to do," then you are in trouble. All these responses indicate that your goals were based on perceived needs, not objective data. I hope you would tell her, "We spent a lot of time examining student data, and it looks as if these are the programs that will reach the right age-groups with the right skills and information before problems start." That answer will make your grandmother, and employer, very proud. Goals must be based on objective data.

Writing Objectives ◄

An **objective** is more precise and time limited than a goal. It specifies a population or a service, a measurable change, and a deadline. Below are some examples of program objectives.

► By June 2002, 300 junior high students will attend training in the Save-a-Lung media awareness program.

► By December 2001, the implementation rate of Safe Friends classroom prevention program in Grades 7 and 8 will be 75%.

Objectives function as a type of checklist toward accomplishing your goals. They clearly and exactly outline all the steps you will take. They also state, in measurable terms, the changes you hope to see in your population. You will be writing both process and outcome objectives.

Process Objectives

Process objectives have to do with implementing your program. They are also called "implementation" objectives. They reflect procedures, purchasing, training, and other program implementation elements. They are easier to write than you might think. Just keep in mind the "rule of fours." Four elements are necessary to include in writing a complete process objective:

1. *What*—Exactly what procedure will be completed?

2. *Who*—Who is the person or group responsible for ensuring that this happens?

3. *How much/how many*—What quantity of this service or procedure, generally expressed as a percentage, will take place?

4. *When*—What is the deadline by which this will have happened?

Let's place these four elements into a sentence. As long as your sentence has all four elements, it is a well-written objective. Look at the following objectives.

▶ By December 2001 (when), 30 (how many) seventh- and eighth-grade teachers (who) will be trained in the Safe Friends classroom prevention program (what).

▶ By June 2002 (when), 10 (how many) students (who) will be trained to present elementary lessons on drug prevention (what).

▶ By June 2002 (when), teachers trained in Safe Friends (who) will have presented 75% (how many) of required lessons (what).

Outcome Objectives

Outcome objectives should describe exactly how you expect the child, population, or group to look after participating in your program. Each objective is just one sentence. Always refer to changes you want to see in your data, both objective data (rates, amounts, and ages) and even subjective data. Yes, changing the perceptions within a given population is a very respectable outcome objective. As is true with process objectives, outcome objectives need to follow the rule of fours. As long as your outcome objective contains these four necessary elements, it will be complete.

TABLE 2.1 Worksheet for Writing Measurable Objectives

Behavior/Attitude	Population	Percent Change	When
Cigar Smoking	Grades 9-10 Female Athletes	50% Decrease	June 2002
Riding With a Drunk Driver	Grades 10-12 Females	50% Decrease	June 2002
Smoking on Campus	Grades 9-12 All Students	20% Decrease	June 2003

Behavior/Attitude. This is often the identified problem you want to change. Make sure this behavior/attitude can be defined and measured. It's difficult to measure statements like "became better parents" and "were more motivated." Exactly what change in behavior or attitude will indicate to you that you have been successful? Be specific.

Population. Who will be changed as a result of this program or intervention—teachers? students? parents? Be specific; mention grade level and gender if appropriate.

Percent Change. By how much do you expect this behavior/attitude to change? Express this as a realistic percentage.

When. By what date do you expect to be able to measure this change?

Sometimes it helps to draw a picture. Use the "Worksheet for Writing Measurable Objectives" (Resource C). If you are working as a larger group, use newsprint to re-create the four-column worksheet with the column headings "Behavior/Attitude," "Population," "Percent Change," and "When." Begin your work by listing real needs in the Behavior/Attitude column. Then indicate the population to be affected (see Table 2.1).

After listing the *what* and *who,* you are halfway to completing your objectives. Now fill in the Percent Change column. Be realistic. Indicate in the When column when you hope to be able to measure this change. This may have to do with the timing of your data collection. Now plug this information into the model behavioral objective in Figure 2.2.

Remember, as long as you stick to the rule of fours and include each of the four necessary elements, you can put them in any order you want and still end up with a measurable objective. Keep it to one sentence if you can.

⚡ FIGURE 2.2. Model Behavioral Objective

> [Behavior/Attitude] among [Population]
>
> will [Percent Change] by [When] .

All four elements in one sentence will result in an objective that is concise and measurable. Here are some examples:

▶ Riding with an intoxicated driver among females, Grades 10 through 12, will decrease by 50% by June 2003.

▶ There will be a 50% decrease in cigar smoking among female athletes in Grades 9 and 10 by June 2002.

▶ Students in Grades 9 through 12 will show a 50% decrease in cigarette smoking on campus by June 2002.

▶ By June 2002, there will be a 25% correction among seventh- to ninth-grade students in the perception that "everyone is smoking marijuana."

Things to Avoid

A few common problems are associated with writing objectives. Let's look at how to fix them.

Vagueness—Lack of Specificity

▶ Kids will stop smoking.

▶ We'll improve school safety.

▶ Students will treat each other with more respect.

These three objectives raise more questions than they answer. Who are the "kids" who are smoking? Where are they smoking—on or off campus? Are you going to improve school environmental or behavioral safety? Improve it how much and by when? What exactly is meant by "respect"? How will this be defined and measured? These vague objectives would be greatly improved by sticking to the rule of fours and specifying who, what, how much, and by when.

Too Specific

▶ By June 2001, rates of student alcohol use to intoxication in Grades 11 and 12 will be reduced by 10% as a result of 10 sessions of classroom instruction in Grades 9 and 10 provided by five counselors trained in the Safe Friends classroom prevention curriculum in 1999.

Just as being too vague is a problem, so is being too specific. How do you know whether your objective is too specific? Use the rule of fours and start counting. If you count more than four elements, then you know you need to rewrite. The above objective looks like three objectives rolled into one. Keep the process objectives separate from the outcome objectives. An objective needs to be taken apart so that process and outcome become clearer.

▶ By December 2001, five school-based counselors will receive training in the Safe Friends classroom-based violence-prevention curriculum. (Process)

▶ By June 2002, 10 sessions of classroom instruction, Grades 9 and 10, will be provided by school-based counselors trained in Safe Friends. (Process)

▶ By June 2003, rates of student-to-student harassment in Grades 11 and 12 will be reduced by 30%. (Outcome)

Here we have three beautiful objectives, two process and one outcome, all following the rule of fours. These objectives are clear, understandable, measurable, and will make program implementation and assessment much simpler.

Often when two or more objectives are combined, you will find the word *and*. If you see that word in your objective, then you may have overwritten it. Take it apart and rewrite it as two or more separate objectives.

Unrealistic

▶ Students in our district will stop using all alcohol and drugs.

It ain't gonna happen. Don't write it down. Avoid universal statements like this one. There is no way to succeed with objectives that are written with the impossible in mind. We certainly want to move in this direction and make as much progress toward non-use as possible, but an objective like this one only ensures failure. Make sure you select a percentage change that you can achieve.

Unmeasurable

▶ Readers will have an increased sense of humor about program development after reading this book.

Make sure the language you use is measurable. This objective isn't easily measured. How do you measure "sense of humor"? Difficult-to-measure qualities include "motivation," "feeling better," and "pride," to name a few. When writing your objectives, refer often to the numbers in your objective data that you would like to see changed after you implement your program. The above objective would be improved if it said, "As a result of reading this book, readers will have reduced levels of stress when working on program development." "Reduced levels of stress" can be measured both physiologically and with valid written inventories.

◢ Developing a Timeline

Once you have reviewed the initial data and have written your goals and objectives, you may be momentarily overwhelmed by what a large job this is becoming. You may be seeing for the first time that the process of developing, implementing, and assessing a prevention program may take 2 to 3 years, not just a few months.

This is where a timeline can be used to relieve some pressure. Timelines break large objectives into smaller, more workable tasks, simplifying the process. They also delegate work and define roles. To create a timeline, you will need a copy of your program objectives and the "Program Timeline" in Resource D. To use this worksheet, begin by inserting the program objectives into the indicated slots (see Table 2.2).

Under each objective, list exactly what must be done to achieve it by the specified date. No task is too small to include. Write in things like trips to the store for supplies, the filling out of forms, making copies, everything that will be involved. This process will help you simplify each objective and delegate responsibilities through your work group.

After you have written down all the tasks necessary to achieve completion of this objective, assign a member of your work group to each task, indicate a date by which each needs to complete this task, and specify any resources the members may need. Once a task has been completed, check it off and move on.

If your group is having regular meetings, review progress on the timeline tasks to check on any hold-ups and what can be done to remedy them. This working timeline will bring together elements of program development, implementation, and the beginnings of your program assessment plan.

TABLE 2.2 Program Timeline

Objective #1: By December 20XX, five school-based counselors will receive training in the Safe Friends classroom-based violence-prevention curriculum.

Tasks	Person Responsible	Resources	Due Date	✔
a. Determine when, where, and the cost of Safe Friends training.	Joe Smith	Phone # of Sponsoring Agency	9-15	
b. Secure funding for training.	Mike James	Copy of Budget	10-30	
c. Arrange stipends, substitute teacher pay, and other miscellaneous expenses.	Mike James	Financial Forms	11-15	
d. Select five counselors to attend training.	Mary Evans		11-15	
e. Attend training.	Counselors	Transportation	12-15	
f. Submit necessary forms for travel and reimbursement.	Counselors	Reimbursement Forms	12-30	

Second Thoughts ◀

▶ Start at the end. When you are writing your program goals and objectives, always keep in mind how you want this population to look after they have received this program; write objectives to get you there.

▶ Remember the differences between real need and perceived need. Programming should be designed on the basis of real need, but changing perceptions could also be a realistic outcome objective.

▶ Remember that goals are broad, umbrella statements of program direction. Objectives specify your population and all the steps you will take to achieve your goal.

▶ Write process and outcome objectives for all programs.

▶ Remember the rule of fours when writing objectives.

Process objectives: What, who, how much/many, and by when.

Outcome objectives: Behavior/attitude, population, percent change, and by when.

▶ Avoid being too specific, too vague, unrealistic, or unmeasurable when writing your objectives.

▶ Reread and rewrite any objective that contains the word *and*. The word is a red flag that signals you may have combined two objectives.

▶ Be specific and realistic. Objectives are the foundation for your program development, implementation, and assessment plan. You will be revisiting them often, and your program success will be measured by your ability to achieve these objectives.

▶ Create a timeline from your objectives to simplify the process of program development, implementation, and eventually program assessment.

Program Review, Selection, and Implementation   3

*It's not only the Colombian cartel that's gotten rich off drugs;
a lot of curriculum marketers are making out like bandits.*

—George H. Bush Administration's
Senior Drug Policy Official

Once you have reviewed the substance use and violence information about
your population and you have established a direction and focus for
program development by writing your goals and objectives, it is time either
to review and revise the programs you are already using or to select and
implement something new (see Figure 3.1).

First, let's look at the programs you are currently using. Where did they
come from? How were they initially selected from the myriad of drug and
violence prevention programs out there? Are they the right programs for
your population and for changing the behaviors you've identified?

Reviewing Current Programs

Too often, drug and violence prevention program decisions are made in late
August, at the end of the fiscal year. It becomes a matter of spending money
so that it doesn't have to be returned. (Plan well so that you never have to
give money back!) Program quality in this situation is a minor concern.
When quick spending decisions are made by the school's fiscal agent and not
by the prevention specialist or an advisory committee, the school ends up
with inadequate and ineffective programs that don't fit its population. Even
when decisions are made more thoughtfully, it's sometimes difficult to find
good information on all the programs out there. Below is a review of some
of the most common sources of program information.

⚡ FIGURE 3.1. Program Development: Flowchart 3

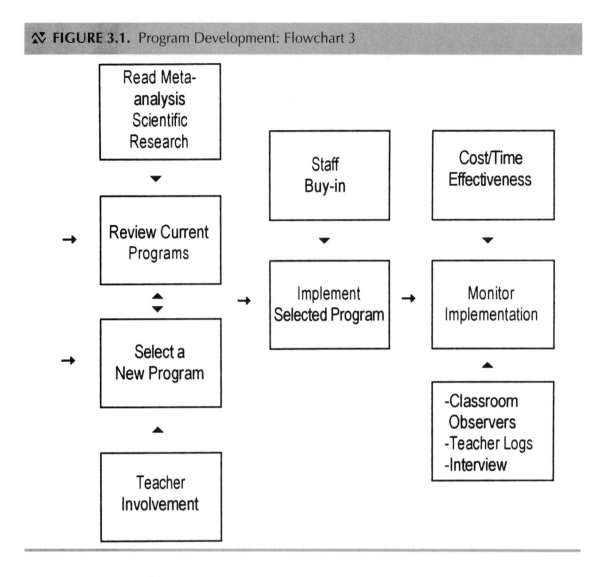

Marketers

Salespeople can be a powerful force. Often, they will come right out to your school. A face-to-face meeting is difficult to resist. That is what program developers are banking on. How easy is it to say no to a real person? Remember that a sales rep, though probably a thoroughly wonderful person you would love to have as a neighbor, is really just a form of advertising, the most engaging and hardest-to-resist kind. *Marketers generally provide you with positive information about their program, not objective information.* Ask marketers whether they can show you evidence of "outcome effectiveness" or some type of scientific proof that their program actually does what it claims to do.

Colleagues

We hear a lot from colleagues about different programs. *This is an important source of information if you want to know how easy a program was to implement or how well their teachers liked it.* Unless they are handing you a study of outcome measures on this program, however, remember that they are not the authority on this program's effectiveness.

Advertisements

Advertisements come in so many forms. They come in very nicely packaged bulk mail, and they're in magazines and even trade and professional journals. Sometimes bookmarks, pens, and other office supplies with the program logo are included. All are designed to increase product recognition. Who doesn't know about DARE? The T-shirts and bumper stickers alone have elevated this program to a household word. But how many people have actually read the original research studies on DARE? Remember that the advertising is not the program. Advertising is like a movie trailer—all the best stuff packed into a 30-second spot. *Product recognition does not equal program effectiveness.*

Program Reviews

Program reviews often accompany marketing materials or appear in magazines or are even included with the program materials. *A review is not an evaluation.* Reviews tend to focus on process elements such as the usability of materials, the ease of integration into a health or general curriculum, the content and quality of the teacher training, the national implementation rates, and student preference for these materials over others. Reviews do not generally address student behavior/attitude change as a result of participating in this program.

Implementation Evaluations

EXAMPLE: One school did the smart thing before spending $20,000 on teacher training and program materials. School personnel contacted the manufacturer and asked whether any evaluation studies had been done. "Oh yes!" the marketer assured them. "We have very extensive data showing tremendous program success. We will be happy to send you the full report." Gee whiz, what could be better? The report they received was indeed extensive. It was nearly 300 pages long. It tracked the number of people trained, the number and type of school districts and grade levels using these materials, and the degree to which trained teachers implemented the program. The school found no mention in this report of whether this program actually changed student attitudes or behaviors.

Implementation statistics that tell you how many schools use the program and how thoroughly the program was implemented are crucial information for program developers and salespeople to have. They reflect the usability of the product. But implementation evaluation doesn't provide a shred of information to a school about how this program might change a student's behaviors and attitudes. *An implementation evaluation is not an evaluation of student outcomes.*

Internet/Web Sites

For some, the Internet is now the fastest and most convenient method of searching for information. *Unfortunately, as we've all found out, the Internet is not a definitive source of accurate information.* Along with the very good sites are many fraudulent and misleading sites. Who sponsors the site? What is the authority of this person or organization? Is there a political or financial reason for this site to be biased? When was the site last revised? Is this site an advertisement disguised as objective information? Use the "Worksheet for Evaluating Web-Based Resources" in Resource E. See Resource F for a partial listing of Web site resources for research-based and science-based prevention programs. Resource G lists additional Web-based substance abuse and violence resources.

Newspapers/Magazines

Just because you read it in the newspaper doesn't mean it's true. The media's job is to report the news that a school has changed programming directions, that teachers will be trained, that a committee has been working all summer, that everyone is very excited about the new program, that we all hope this program will reduce the identified problem. It's possible that the newspaper article isn't objective. Remember that the field of violence and substance abuse prevention can be extremely political and emotional. Sometimes people will even intentionally "spin" data to capture headlines. Occasionally, a newspaper article will report on research about a specific program. I have seen this with the popular DARE program. With every new research study on prevention, articles in the popular press generally mention DARE. *Publicity does not equal effectiveness.* In this case, follow the references mentioned and read the original piece of research yourself.

Television/Radio

Some prevention programs are high profile enough that you will hear about them on television or radio. They may be in the news because of the visibility of program implementation (e.g., rallies, parades, public artwork), or prevention advertisements may be sponsored by certain programs. *Publicity does not equal effectiveness.* Quite a few high-profile programs have never been proved effective. If what you hear about a program on television or radio interests you, go to a more reputable source of information to see whether this prevention program is indeed effective.

Editorials/Letters

Editorials and letters are generally opinion, a vehicle for theoretical discussions, not fact. Two case history letters to reputable medical journals (a 1972 letter to the *New England Journal of Medicine* and a 1980 letter to the *Journal of Pediatrics*) discussed males with breast enlargement or delayed puberty who also were marijuana smokers. Although breast enlargement caused by marijuana smoking has never been confirmed through research, that didn't stop the misinterpretation of a letter as "fact," resulting in the widely held but inaccurate belief that smoking pot causes men to grow breasts. Editorials and letters are opinion, not fact.

Government Reports

Government reports can run the spectrum from excellent to useless. Some government reports have been written to showcase government-funded programs whether they were evaluated or not. Most recently, though, some of the best resources for evaluation of effectiveness have been literature reviews and meta-analyses produced by government agencies. Check the date on the report you are reading. Most government reports since "Principles of Effectiveness" (U.S. Department of Education, 1998b) have been extremely useful, research-based, objective sources of information on prevention program effectiveness.

Case Studies

Case studies are subjective (not objective) reports of a series of events or experiences. They are descriptive rather than evaluative. Often full of details, they describe the experience of a group or a person (a "case") with a particular prevention program or combination of interventions. Case studies are a great source for generating ideas, program improvements, and research design ideas and for identifying possible variables for targeting programs. *Case studies are not a reliable source of information on program effectiveness.* The generally small group size and the more subjective nature of these reports make the transfer of results from their case to your situation invalid.

Testimonials

"Well, I went through that program, and I never got involved with drugs, so it must be great!" We've all heard them. In some situations, testimonials are very powerful and persuasive. Remember that problems of violence, alcohol, tobacco, and other drug use are very complex and that all students are individuals. *Testimonials are not proof that a program is effective.* If you hear many testimonials about one particular program, then you may want to find an evaluation study on that program.

Committee Reports

Your school's Health Advisory Committee might recommend one program over another. Find out what criteria they used to arrive at this recommendation. Are they recommending this particular program because it is inexpensive? Because other area schools are using it? Because it's easy to implement? Although these are valid points, they are not the best reasons for selecting a program. Did they review data, target goals and objectives, and then review evaluation studies to arrive at their final recommendations? If so, then accept their recommendations.

Student/Participant Feedback

After programs and workshops, assemblies and trainings, you hand your students or participants a "feedback" form. (See the "Sample Youth Participant Feedback Sheet" in Resource H and the "Sample Adult Participant Feedback Sheet" in Resource I.) Responses are generally recorded on a Likert-type, strongly agree/strongly disagree scale. This is probably the first and last feedback you get on your event. These are not measures of program effectiveness. However, this information is very important "process" feedback. On the basis of this participant feedback, you may choose to hold the event in a different room or at a different time of day or time of year, make it longer or shorter, use different trainers, or add more activities. *This information will help you improve program implementation; it is not a measure of program effectiveness.*

Scientific Research

Scientific research is published in professional journals. Professional journals generally publish quarterly or bimonthly. They publish some articles and editorials, but mostly clinical studies. Many journals are peer-reviewed, which means that all research submitted is reviewed by a committee of professionals for experimental design, methodology, and data collection. Only after a piece of research passes the peer-review process—and not all do—does it appear in the journal. This process ensures that the research you read is based on sound scientific methods and allows valid conclusions to be drawn. *This is the best place to find evaluation studies on programs you are considering.* You may want to check with your local university library to see which journals it has.

All these sources of information are important because they will provide you with information about program content, program acceptance, and general public attitudes about this intervention. *Remember that the only resource that is a valid source of information on program effectiveness is scientific research.* Other, nonscientific sources of information often contain references to research so that you can look up the original clinical evaluation.

More than a decade of solid research is available on what makes a program effective in preventing drug use or violent behavior. The easiest way to select an effective program is to refer to one of the meta-analyses or summarized program lists that have been written since 1998. These lists have identified programs with research-based or science-based effectiveness (see Resource F).

The Education Development Center (EDC) has collected and reviewed evaluations of the research on drug and violence prevention. It has published a resource that lists 29 programs by title, objective, target population, duration, costs, strategy, required training, and outcomes. This list continues to grow as program developers submit their evaluation research. You can receive a copy of the current EDC list of effective prevention programs by contacting the Education Development Center (www.edc.org).

The Center for the Study of Prevention of Violence has developed "blueprints" for 10 exemplary violence prevention programs. All programs listed show an experimental design, evidence (statistically significant) of participant behavior change, evidence that this change lasted more than 1 year, and successful replication with consistent results. These are very high standards for program effectiveness. You can find these at http.www.colorado.edu/cspv.blueprints/.

Drug Strategies has done an excellent job of staying on top of drug and violence prevention programs. It has two very helpful publications: *Making the Grade: A Guide to School Drug Prevention Programs* (1999) and *Safe Schools, Safe Students: A Guide to Violence Prevention Strategies* (1998). First published in 1996, *Making the Grade* reviews the 50 most widely used prevention programs, including information on cost, teacher training, developmental appropriateness, and fidelity of implementation. It also discusses and compares 14 programs that have undergone rigorous evaluation. *Safe Schools, Safe Students* is a similar collection and review of the 84 most popular violence prevention programs, including 11 that have undergone evaluation studies.

Implementing a New Program ◀

You would think that the difficult part was behind you by the time you have collected and reviewed all the data, established goals, written objectives, and selected appropriate programs. But for your selected program to be effective, you will have to take great care in implementation.

It is necessary to implement your program in exactly the same way that it was demonstrated to be effective. Changes made in implementation will change your results. The rule of thumb with program implementation is "no shortcuts."

Training. If a full-day teacher training is required, do it that way. Don't try to save time and money by boiling 7 hours of material into a 2-hour workshop. There is a reason why the training is 7 hours long. There is a reason why all those activities are included. Provide the training as prescribed because that is how it was found to be effective (Scheirer & Rezmovic, 1982).

Sessions/Length. If the curriculum includes 15 classroom lessons, then all 15 need to be presented. If only 8 to 10 are presented, then you are compromising the effectiveness of the program.

Target Early. Implement early, before the behavior you are trying to prevent begins. Often before students participate in a program, they have already formed basic attitudes or have begun negative behaviors. Day-late programs are remedial, not preventive. Remedial prevention programs are less effective. It's more difficult to change established attitudes and behaviors than it is to prevent their formation in the first place (Goplerup, 1991).

Timing/Scheduling. If the program is designed as a 3-day student retreat, doing it as 1 hour after school each week for a semester significantly changes its design. If you redesign the program format, don't expect the same results.

Teaching. If the program is supposed to be led by a counselor, have a counselor lead it. If it's supposed to be peer led, make sure to use peers. This is how it demonstrated effectiveness, so don't modify this design.

Materials. Use the materials as they are. Removing things and adding things change the integrity of the program and may reduce its effectiveness.

Mix-'n'-Match. Taking good elements from several different research-based programs and recombining them for classroom use really constitutes developing an entirely new program. Although those elements were all part of research-based programs, they have probably not been evaluated as stand-alone items. By recombining, you are essentially creating a whole new program that has not been evaluated for effectiveness.

Monitoring. Stay in close touch with the staff who are implementing the program. Routinely observe and talk with them to determine the ease and extent of program implementation. Do whatever troubleshooting is necessary without making significant changes in the program's content, duration, or integrity. Contact the program creators if you're not sure about changes you may have to make.

Stick as closely as you can to the recommended implementation as prescribed by the program creators. Sometimes it may seem needlessly complicated, cumbersome, or labor-intensive. The alternative, making changes and compromising program effectiveness, is undesirable. Take no shortcuts with implementation (Blakely, Emshoff, & Roitman, 1984).

Monitoring Program Implementation ◀

> **EXAMPLE:** One school implemented a nationally recognized drug prevention program. School personnel were extremely disappointed 2 years later when their data showed no change in student risk behaviors or use behaviors. They initially concluded that this national program simply wasn't effective with their population of students. A closer look revealed that implementation at the classroom level had been poor. Content and activities had been randomly eliminated by teachers because of time constraints. The most accurate conclusion that could be drawn was that students hadn't actually received this national program because implementation was so incomplete. Effectiveness of this program could not be measured.

This case certainly begs the question, How do you ensure faithful classroom implementation of a new program? In addition to motivating the teaching staff and providing thorough staff development surrounding your new program, you must have staff buy-in. In fact, buy-in might be the most crucial factor predicting your success or failure with a new program.

Facilitating Staff Buy-In

Without staff buy-in, program implementation will be incomplete. No staff member likes to be "surprised" with curriculum add-ons or told what to do and how to do it without having some say of his or her own. If you do not provide for staff involvement from the very beginning, then you are compromising the effectiveness and completeness of program implementation.

It's important that the staff who will be using these new programs be included in the process that precedes material selection. By involving them in the initial data review and the writing of program goals and objectives, they will have a better understanding of what the current student risk behaviors are, what needs to change, and how the school plans to do this. They can also be involved in selecting the new curriculum or program. They will have a better picture of their role and the importance of that role. They will know what format will work best for their teaching style and student population and what will work best within the school structure. Once materials are selected, they can help schedule intensive staff training as necessary.

Before presenting changes to your staff or community, consider the following thoughts about the process of change.

Take Your Time

Change is a process; it takes time. Your staff won't swing over and embrace your ideas after a 30-minute meeting. Rather than get angry at how slow the process can be, anticipate it.

How. Having your staff involved with the short- and long-term planning will facilitate this change. Start the process 6 months earlier than you think you need to.

Meet Their Needs

"How will I benefit from this?" "What's in it for me?" If you want staff buy-in, then you need to meet staff needs rather than expect them to meet yours.

How. Is there an advantage to doing things the new way? Make sure everyone can see that advantage. Also make sure staff know that there is a reason for the change, that there will be compensation or support for them if they have to change their routine, and that there will be adequate training provided in the new materials or techniques. Ask what would make things easier and how you can help, and then follow through with what is agreed on. Listen carefully when they talk and especially when they complain.

Speak Their Language

The more you speak the language of your staff or community group, the easier it will be for them to hear your ideas. Keep your information relevant to your audience.

How. When talking with teachers, explain the educational impact of this change or program. When talking with community groups, explain the impact of this change or program on local business, community climate, or juvenile crime rates. You may want a member of the specific population you will be addressing to give the actual presentation or "pitch" the program.

Keep Change Small and Simple

When new programming comes to schools, staff are pulled out of their comfort zones and are expected to change personal habits and reschedule their days and sometimes their entire curriculum. Your proposed changes need to be small.

How. Present it as something that is similar to what is already being done. The closer the change is to current behavior or practice, the easier it will be to accept. The less effort that is required to change, the more likely it will be that change will happen.

Growth Is Required

Change requires growth. In this case, that means having a clear understanding of current alcohol, drug, and violence types and rates in the population to be served by this program; thorough training in the new materials; and crystal clear and irrefutable reasons for everyone doing this.

How. It is a good idea to involve key staff with data collection and review from the very beginning. Let everyone discover the problems that exist together and be part of the decision making about program changes.

Everyone Is Different

People will accept change at different speeds. Some will jump right on the bandwagon, some will be slow to agree or will agree with conditions, some will require support through the change process, and a few will resist until the bitter end and may even act as saboteurs.

How. Remember to listen and keep an honest dialogue going. Open and honest communication is your best defense against the naysayers.

Change Is Reversible

All changes are ultimately reversible. You can always go back to the old way if the new way doesn't work.

How. Remind all involved parties that the reason you are evaluating is to make sure these changes are worth all the trouble. If they're not, they won't last.

Maintain Change

Maintaining change takes constant effort until it becomes habit. During this initial period, the staff must be supported and motivated to continue moving in the new direction. Without support, there may be relapse to older and easier ways.

How. Be a constant presence. Ask how the new program is working; provide support in the form of time, materials, or stipends for training or overtime.

Minimize the Risks

Who exactly is responsible if this program fails? Who will be held accountable, and what will be the impact on the school and community? The lower the personal risk, the more likely people will be to accept change.

How. Specifically outline who is accountable for program selection, materials acquisition, program scheduling, and implementation and evaluation of program effectiveness. Also outline the costs (energy, time, money) if this fails and indicate that it is worth the risk. Explain the track record and reputation of the selected program.

Implementation Evaluation

Evaluating how thoroughly and accurately a program has been implemented is a necessary part of program development. Implementation evaluation is based mostly on observation and interviews. You are trying to determine to what extent the selected program was implemented and with what accuracy of content. Ideally, you will find that program leaders are able to cover all the material in the prescribed order and within the budgeted time and cost allowances.

Classroom Observers. To evaluate program implementation, you need someone to visit classrooms to observe how implementation is taking place. This person can observe the classroom lessons while using the "Sample Classroom Observation Sheet" (Resource J), interview teachers or students, and compare how one teacher may be doing things differently from another teacher. It's best if this person is neutral.

Teacher Implementation Logs. Have teachers, program presenters, or facilitators keep logs of times, dates, glitches, and what material was or was not covered for each session. Use the "Sample Teacher Implementation Log" in Resource K. Review these implementation logs to determine whether program leaders were able to stick with the prescribed content and timeline.

Interviews. Conduct mid- and postprogram interviews with program leaders. Ask about schedules and ease of implementation, satisfaction with content, and suggestions for improvements.

Cost/Time Effectiveness. Determine cost/time effectiveness of the program. Was it within budget? (See Chapter 7 and all samples and worksheets in Resources T and U.)

Feedback. Use the "Sample En-Route Participant Feedback" form (Resource L) to get information from participants, their thoughts and feelings on what it was like to participate in this program. Also get feedback from the teachers or program facilitators. Is there an easier way of doing this? A better place to hold the program? Can it be done with fewer program leaders? With different materials?

Remember, always check with the program creators before making any major changes in the implementation design. If you do end up making significant changes, make sure you have a comparison group so that you can determine whether your changes had a negative or positive effect on program effectiveness. Use of comparison groups and other types of experimental designs are discussed in later chapters.

Second Thoughts ◀

▶ Examine sources of information on program effectiveness to make sure the program is objective and research based.

▶ Use more than one source for program information when making program selection decisions. The Internet is not definitive.

▶ Develop an understanding of how to facilitate change.

▶ Implement your program exactly as it was designed.

▶ Contact program creators first for feedback and additional ideas if you need to make changes in program content or format.

▶ Evaluate your program implementation.

4 Creating Homegrown Programs

Elements of Effective Prevention

Science is always simple and always profound. It is only the half-truths that are dangerous.
—G. B. Shaw, 1913, *The Doctor's Dilemma*

Maybe you can't find a packaged program that addresses the needs or the population you've identified, and you think you might have to develop your own program. Maybe you are currently using a homegrown program. This chapter reviews what is currently known about effective violence and substance abuse prevention techniques and how you can incorporate them into the development of your own homegrown prevention program to increase its effectiveness.

It is crucial that the person who will be writing the program curriculum or the student materials be an expert in substance abuse or violence prevention. This will minimize the risks of creating programs and materials that backfire—or actually do more harm than good. Having an interest in trying to write a prevention curriculum is not a replacement for a strong general methods course and thorough familiarity with current research on what is and is not effective prevention.

Perhaps most important of all, *you must stay current*. I can't stress this point enough. Prevention programs have failed in the past because they were based on faulty assumptions about why young people engage in risky behaviors and what types of programming actually changes behavior. There is no way around this. If you don't do the reading and don't look for proven methods, techniques, and program designs, you may end up wasting a lot of time and money by developing and implementing a program that doesn't work. Many current federal documents (see Resource M) and listservs for dialoguing with other substance abuse and violence prevention professionals (see Resource N) are on-line.

If you don't believe that you can adhere to these suggestions, then you may be better off looking for a program that has already been developed, field-tested, or evaluated. Although the satisfaction of writing your own program may be great, and you know that the final product will be an excellent fit with your population, there can be no shortcuts when developing a new program.

Effective Prevention Programming

Target All Use

Avoid drug-of-the-month or fad-focused formats. Instead target your programming to broader behaviors that are precursors to substance use and violence (see Resource O). A curriculum or program that is specific to "crack use" or "firearm possession" will not be appropriate for your general population.

Implement Early, Before Behavior Begins

The definition of *prevention* is to prevent a particular behavior or pattern of behaviors from starting. This means that successful prevention programming must begin early enough in the socialization process to provide direction in development, prevent the occurrence of root causes, and deter antecedent or precursor behaviors. Programs implemented too late, or after risk behaviors begin, are remedial rather than preventive. Remedial programs are less likely to be effective because it's more difficult to change established attitudes and behaviors than it is to prevent their initial formation.

An elementary-based prevention program plays a critical role in the prevention of disease, reduction of addictions and other risk behaviors, later health problems, and psychopathology. One necessary goal for early substance abuse prevention programs is to delay first use. The odds of lifetime alcohol abuse and dependence increase for each decreasing year of age of initiation. That means the younger they are when they start, the more likely they are to become addicted later in life (Clark, Kirisi, & Tater, 1998). Delaying first use of tobacco products is especially critical because the older you are when you start smoking, the greater your success will be in eventually quitting. In addition, adolescent onset of substance abuse is correlated with higher psychopathology rates, including conduct disorders and major depression (U.S. Department of Justice, 2000).

Violence prevention is a little trickier. The risk factors for violent behavior are more age and stage specific. For example, some violence prevention programs promote peer acceptance as a necessary protective factor. This tactic is effective in the elementary grades but might backfire in middle and high school, depending on the peers. Violence prevention has to be very carefully tailored to a student's developmental stage (Hawkins et al., 2000). Successful programs will have early and sustained intervention.

Ongoing, Long-Term, With Booster Sessions

The prevention message needs to be longer than just 3 to 5 weeks. Some evaluations of 16-week programs showed that student behavior change occurred during the course of the program but that once it was over, behavior returned to preprogram levels. Your programming needs to be in place throughout the school year, from elementary grades through high school. Repeat the message, develop booster sessions, and focus on student grade-level transitions and building transitions (Botvin et al., 1989; Rosenbaum et al., 1994; Sherman et al., 1997).

Multiage, Not Just Implemented at One Grade Level

When is the "right" grade level to talk about drugs or violence? It depends on the readiness and developmental level of each child. To ensure that you reach all children, the prevention message needs to be multiage. Different prevention messages and skills need to be taught as children mature through their developmental stages.

Keep Content Developmentally Appropriate

Keep reading level, content, activities, and program structure developmentally appropriate. At the elementary level, the developmental task is prosocial bonding. Arrange programs so that elementary students have a chance to interact in mixed groups. At the middle school level, the developmental focus is on social success and social influence. Group projects and teaming will be most effective at this age and stage. Identity formation is the developmental focus of high school students. They will respond to leadership, being Big Brothers or Big Sisters, and volunteerism. Structure programs that meet your students where they are developmentally.

Comprehensive, Integrated Within the Curriculum and School Structure

Stand-alone programs have never been very effective. Many violence and substance abuse prevention programs are add-on, disparate elements of a school experience, rather than well-planned, integral parts of a comprehensive prevention curriculum or program. By isolating drug and violence prevention education from the general curriculum and putting it into separate weekly lessons for only part of a semester, you effectively remove that information from the general learning experience. By separating this material from practical application in other learning areas, you also reduce the student's ability to transfer knowledge and skills to "real life" situations (Elias & Clabby, 1984; Goplerup, 1991).

A truly comprehensive program will take place not only in the classrooms but also on the athletic fields and in the principal's office. It will be written into school policy, teachers will receive training updates, and parents and community members will be involved.

Think about how the American Heart Association promoted the messages about reducing the risk for heart disease by changing exercise and diet. The message was everywhere and all the time. It was on television, on the radio, on billboards, in buses, on park benches, on little informational slips tucked into your Visa bill. It was on the poster in your doctor's office. The same poster was at your gym, and even restaurant menus started identifying "heart healthy" foods. The prevention message was everywhere, and this comprehensive approach was successful in making all of us aware of the behavior changes we needed to make to reduce our risk for heart disease. When you design your prevention program, think broadly and comprehensively.

Skill-Based, Practical Strategies

Students know the information. What they need are skills for integrating that information into their choices. Skills need to be broad-based life skills, not just refusal skills.

With substance abuse, peer pressure rarely takes the form of direct solicitation. Children may learn to "just say no" and then have nowhere to use that skill. Teaching refusal skills alone isn't practical or effective. Students are more likely to be presented with the opportunity to use when they are in groups where others are using and they feel drawn to conform. Conforming is a necessary developmental task for achieving social success. It's difficult to compete with how humans are hard-wired, so don't try. Teach them how to identify their own feelings, values, and beliefs as separate from those of the crowd. Teach the skills for handling tricky, awkward, or dangerous social situations. Acknowledge that it is very difficult not to go along with their friends at this age (Botvin et al., 1989).

Specific skills have been connected with the prevention of hate crimes, prejudice, sexism, and racism: anger management, empathy and perspective taking, peace building (building and maintaining positive relationships), negotiation and problem solving, skills for handling situations that involve teasing and bullying, and active listening skills (Sherman et al., 1997).

Violence prevention skills also need to include specific information on the role of bystanders as enhancers or reducers of conflict. Students will not learn these skills from media coverage of crimes of hate, bias, and violence because, in general, bystanders are not helpful in the de-escalation of these events.

By teaching students relevant, practical skills of self-control, goal setting, and dealing with stress, you are teaching violence and drug prevention (Brewer, et al., 1995; Lipsey, 1992).

Time for Practice, Practice, Practice

Teaching the skill is not enough. Some research on skill acquisition suggests that students need close to 50 hours of rehearsal or practice time before they will actually use their new skills outside the classroom (Connell, Turner, & Mason, 1985). To get that sort of practice time into a standard curriculum, the skills have to be integrated across the curriculum so that they can be practiced and reinforced in different environments throughout the day.

Multiple Learning Styles

Not every student learns the same way. For programming to reach the widest population of students, it needs to be targeted to all learning styles, including any special education or resource room students you might be serving. Avoid straight lecture; make use of interactive and varied teaching methods. See Resource P for more information on effective teaching and organizational methods.

Teacher Training

The research on teacher training is very conclusive. Statistically significant differences in student risk behaviors have been found between students whose teachers had intensive staff development and students whose teachers had just inservice training or nothing at all. Teachers who received intensive training in drug prevention or drug prevention curricula had classrooms of students with lower rates of risk behaviors. Staff development for all levels of caretakers is a wise expenditure of funds (Allison, Silverman, & Dignam, 1990).

Clarify and Correct Perceptions

Sometimes students will tell you that they do something because "everyone else is doing it." Students rarely discuss this with each other, and the media reinforce these inaccurate beliefs. In fact, most data on drug use and violence suggest that the students who are involved are the minority. Most students are *not* doing it, not even close.

Additionally, increased perceptions that their friends are intolerant of drug use and violent behavior is key to reducing these behaviors. If students think their friends won't approve, they are much less likely to engage in the behavior.

Students need to understand that violence and drug use are not the norm. Clarifying with students can go a long way toward relieving them of the pressure to conform to the perceived majority (Hansen & Graham, 1991; Institute of Medicine, 1994).

Involve Family and Community

Family involvement is the single greatest predictor of success in substance abuse treatment. Community support is crucial for the message of non-use and nonviolence to be truly comprehensive and community-wide. A solid parent-family focused component will reinforce messages being taught at school and will increase open family discussion on topics of substance abuse and violence (*Preventing Drug Use Among Children and Adolescents*, 1997).

Make Physical Changes

Physical changes in the environment are particularly important when your program objectives are to reduce precursors to violence. Look around the physical spaces on campus. Increase illumination of poorly lit or obscured places. Clean the place up. With student help, a coat of fresh paint and a clean parking lot and grounds will go a long way toward improving school climate and student mood. Allow the students ownership. Even if they have color choices and ideas that offend some adults, a sense of ownership of the building and grounds will lead to reduced vandalism (see Resource O).

Consider Policy Changes

Ensure that the school policies are up to date and support any and all changes in curriculum, training, and other programming (Burk, 1998). Policies that demonstrate respect for students rather than being strictly punitive are more effective in achieving peaceful and healthy norms. Policies must also have clear procedures that need to be enforced in a consistent, visible, and immediate way to ensure that they are effective in deterring certain behaviors (Gottfredson, Gottfredson, & Hybl, 1993).

> **EXAMPLE:** Before rewriting the school's substance abuse policy, a group of students was assembled to provide feedback on what they did and did not like about the old policy. One particular problem came up: Students said they had no way to refer a teammate whom they might have concerns about without that teammate getting suspended from play. There was also no way for a team member to seek help without getting suspended from play. They thought any person should be able to seek medical help without fear of punishment. As written, the policy actually worked against the health and wellness of team members. The students suggested that a clause be included in the new policy to allow for one-time amnesty from

discipline for a student who asks for help with a drug or alcohol problem—as long as that student follows through with the recommended treatment. This policy inclusion led to higher rates of identification of students who needed help with drug and alcohol problems, improved follow-through with recommended treatment, kept them connected to their teams and activities, and improved communication between students and the coaching staff.

Things to Avoid

Information Only

For decades, we taught students the facts about drugs. We showed them what they looked like, how much they cost, and how it felt to use them. Information-only programs like this did not reduce drug use behavior then, and they won't work now. Statistics indicate that when we provide all this information, we reduce fear and contribute to *increases* in drug use behavior. Fact-based prevention programming walks a thin line between prevention and promotion, depending on what and how facts are shared (Botvin, 1990).

There was actually a time in the 1970s when officials at the then leading drug abuse agency for the federal government, the Special Action Office for Drug Abuse Prevention (SAODAP), concluded that misinformation and negative effects were too widespread. They imposed a temporary ban on federal funding of fact-based drug information materials because these were considered counterproductive to the larger goals of reducing substance use (Resnick, 1990).

We taught students information about the signs and symptoms of addiction, as well as identification, intervention, and recovery. This also did not reduce substance use. It was like teaching CPR as a way of promoting heart disease prevention. We had it backward.

Scare Tactics

Scare tactics are ineffective in achieving reductions in use or changes in risk behavior. Scare tactics seem like a logical idea, but they have been shown to have no lasting impact on changing student behaviors. In fact, some susceptible youth who witness graphic media violence intended to "scare" them away from violent behavior may become more likely to be violent themselves. A few students may actually make lifetime changes in behavior as a result of the graphic drunk driving assembly, but most will not. Scare tactics may be effective as short-term safety programs for drunk driving, but not much else (Botvin, 1990).

Moralizing

Moralizing, or telling children that their behavior must change because it is wrong or immoral, is also not effective. In fact, speaking to children this way sounds punitive and will limit or end open conversation. Teaching moral behaviors is done best through example, not lecture (Botvin, 1990).

Self-Esteem Programming

The urge to boost self-esteem to reduce risk behaviors is a natural one. Research shows, however, that self-esteem changes do not result in behavior changes and that when they do, they are often in the opposite direction! Most self-esteem research has been correlational, not showing cause-effect relationships, so the conclusions that connect self-esteem to drug use behavior are not correct. Self-esteem programs designed as violence prevention are showing themselves to be consistently ineffective because many aggressive and violent youth have very high self-esteem (Botvin, 1990; Scheirer & Kraut, 1979; Schroeder, Laflin, & Weis, 1993).

Grouping High-Risk Youth

Grouping high-risk youth for specialized programming has had ineffective and even disastrous results (Gottfredson, 1987). With substance abusers, the group norm of use becomes higher than in the general student population. All group behavior will move toward the group norm, resulting in *higher* rates of drug use. If you've ever put all your student smokers together in a room, held weekly smoking cessation groups, and then wondered why, after 3 months, everyone was still smoking or smoking more, now you know. You did not fail; you were a victim of group dynamics. Grouping aggressive or antisocial students for specialized programming will also establish a negative peer group with group norms that will lead to higher rates of aggressive behaviors. Some alternative education programs are discovering these rules of group dynamics the hard way.

Conclusion

Whether you are reviewing current programs, purchasing new programs, or planning to write your own, seek out evaluation studies that show how this program, method, or technique changes student attitudes and behaviors. Be aware of sources of non-objective data. Once you have your program ready to go, implement faithfully, exactly as recommended, without cutting corners.

Evaluation studies make your work easier and more difficult at the same time. By narrowing your choices of materials, methods, and populations, you have fewer and easier decisions to make. But faithful implementation of an evaluated program can be difficult. It requires accurate attention to detail and total follow-through.

Remember that you will have to prove to your school, community, and the state and federal sources of your funding that the program you are using or have created is effective in changing student attitudes and behaviors. Keep this in mind as you make all your material and program decisions.

▣ Second Thoughts

▶ Substance use and violence are complex human behaviors. Programming must address both individual and social/institutional influences.

▶ Programming is strongest when not a stand-alone or add-on, but an integral part of the school curriculum reflected in general organization, practices, policies, and school climate.

▶ The prevention message is reinforced across grade levels and subject areas.

▶ No single strategy, alone, has ever demonstrated long-term impact.

▶ *Comprehensive* doesn't mean "more"; it means identifying the different types of variables and attending to them.

▶ If you will be writing your own program, do your reading and adhere to current research on best practices in prevention.

Additional Data Collection 5

Preparing for Assessment of Program Effectiveness

Not everything that can be counted counts: and not everything that counts can be counted.

—Albert Einstein

Thorough data collection will be the cornerstone for assessing your program's effectiveness. It's never too early to begin collecting additional data on your students. In a perfect world, you will know every possible thing there is to know about your population before developing and implementing your prevention program. Unfortunately, that's not how it really works; we simply do not have the time to tirelessly collect data. In this chapter, you will learn that it's in your best interest to collect broader data than what was needed in Chapter 2 to determine your program goals and write your objectives. It's a good idea to collect as many population-specific data as you have the time for, because although it may not matter now, it will matter later.

> **EXAMPLE:** The High/Scope Perry Preschool Project (U.S. Department of Justice, 2000) is one of the more successful and enduring early childhood programs. It was originally designed as an educational **intervention** for students at high risk for academic failure. Years of broad baseline data collection has allowed identification of additional positive program outcomes that go far beyond academic success. These outcomes include (a) reduced out-of-wedlock births, (b) reduced arrests for dealing drugs, (c) reduced multiple arrests and juvenile delinquency, and (d) reduced misconduct, fighting, and other violent behaviors. Not only does this program work to prevent academic failure, but it is a violence and delinquency prevention program as well. The data easily show proof of program effectiveness. As a result, funding becomes available from additional sources, which allows this excellent program to continue and expand services to even more youth and families.

⚡ FIGURE 5.1. Program Development: Flowchart 4

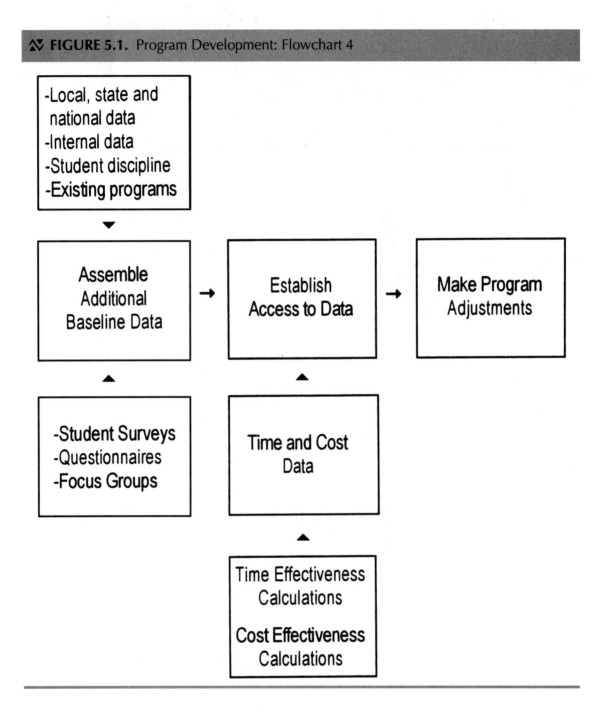

A year after you first implement your program, you will take another look at your baseline and **comparison data** (see the process in Figure 5.1). This is how you will know whether the program you are using is actually changing the behaviors of your students. If you have collected broad enough data, then you may find that not only did your program reduce indicators of drug use or violence but it may have resulted in changes in other risk behaviors as well.

EXAMPLE: Personnel at one school did a thorough data collection, implemented a drug prevention program, and then re-collected their baseline data 1 year later. They were disappointed that the program's effect on drug use behaviors had been so minor. Closer examination of the data, however, showed a remarkable increase in student seat belt and helmet use! Where did that come from? Did their programming have the unexpected effect of changing student safety behaviors? They were very happy with this unanticipated outcome and glad they had collected the initial data. Without such a thorough initial data collection, this change might have gone unnoticed.

Baseline Data ◀

Baseline data generally means the initial data against which all future data will be measured to determine the direction and magnitude of change. To show change over time, you must have something from the very beginning against which to compare your current data. If you are starting a diet, you generally weigh in during the first week. How else would you know whether you lost or gained weight without this initial measurement? That weigh-in during the first week of your diet is your baseline measurement.

Data displays that show rates of drug use or violence in a particular population are not very useful unless you have a basis for comparison. What does it mean to say that marijuana use in your school is at 12%? Is that high or low? Is that an improvement, or are things getting worse? It is important to provide either baseline data from the same population or similar data from another population as a comparison to make your data meaningful.

EXAMPLE: One large city district published an extensive document on student drug use and violence trends. A group of school personnel had been collecting the substance abuse data for nearly a decade and had made graphs showing decreases over time. The data were encouraging and well presented. However, the data on violence were misleading. Because the staff had nothing to compare the data to, they had simply created a table that showed the actual number of weapon incidents. It would have been more meaningful if they could have provided what these numbers represented per capita (which was far less than 1%) or provided some comparison with state or national data. Even better would have been a comparison with data from other city schools of similar size across the country.

In addition to baseline measures of drug use and violent behaviors, you may also want to collect data on precursor behaviors. These are the risk behaviors seen before the drug use and violence begin (Gottfredson, Sealock, & Koper, 1996; Hawkins et al., 2000) (see Resource O). Ideally, you will be targeting your prevention programs early enough to affect these precursor behaviors.

Also to be gathered are data on demographic risk factors such as neighborhood of residence, family composition, and socioeconomic status. Even though these factors cannot be changed by school-based programming, these demographic data are still necessary to collect for two reasons. First, they will help you understand the population you are serving so that you can develop better programs. Second, these demographic data will strengthen all your grants and other requests for funding.

Define Your Terms

Know What You're Measuring

How come one agency reports 10 violent community incidents, but another in the same town reports 210? You may have discovered that what one agency records as a "violent incident" is defined very differently from how another agency defines a "violent incident." For this reason, the data you collect from different places may not match. It's all about how the terms and behaviors were defined before the counting began.

It is important for you to *define your terms* before you begin so that you know exactly what you're measuring and how to collect the data. For example, if you will be collecting data on the number of verbal outbursts or talking back, then you must first define exactly what does and does not constitute a "verbal outburst." Second, you must devise a system for collecting those data with classroom teachers. This might include teaching teachers to be more aware, devising a form for written feedback, or implementing a new type of behavioral referral system. Define your terms clearly at the beginning so that you and everyone else involved knows how to count what it is you are counting.

Target Population

You will also need to define clearly your **target population** before you begin collecting your data. Carefully describe the population that is the recipient of your programming. Include in this description their age, race, gender, cultural background, and any other relevant identifiers. Write this down so that it can be shared with everyone involved. It is possible that once you collect and compare your data, you will decide that a different target population is actually in need of programming.

Collect Your Data

National Data

Collect local, regional, state, and national data. It's always a good idea to compare your local data with the broader national population so that you can see whether changes are resulting from local programming or are simply reflecting national trends. Some places to start collecting national youth data can be found in Resource Q.

Here's how to use national data. The 1998 National Household Survey on Drug Abuse (NHSDA, 1998) reports that 8.3% of students aged 12 to 17 are current users of marijuana. If your local student survey shows that marijuana use among the same age-group is at 5.2%, then you can congratulate yourselves on having a lower than national rate of marijuana use. However, if your local statistics also show that the marijuana use rate in 1996-97 was at 2.6%, then your use rate has doubled even though the figure is not quite as high as the national average. Find sources of national data that correspond to the local data you are collecting.

Statewide Data

Most states have offices that collect statewide data on substance abuse and other specific youth issues. Start your search for statewide data by looking in the Government Listings section of your local telephone book. Try the state office of alcoholism or its equivalent, statewide cancer and lung associations, state education department, state youth bureau, state department of health, state administrative office of the courts, and state census. Most of these organizations maintain data on youth behavior trends, and often it takes just a telephone call to receive a copy. Don't stop there. Contact any state department or agency that provides services to youth. Use these data in the same way you would use national data.

Regional Data

Often states will provide data broken down by regions, or "service areas." You can also collect your own regional data. Local hospitals, county-wide service agencies, colleges, and universities often have projects or grants that require the collection of regional youth data. The best way to find this sort of regional data is to ask around and make telephone calls.

One school found that a local cancer treatment facility had accumulated more than 5 years of student data on tobacco use patterns. Another school made calls to local colleges and found a graduate student who was doing a research project on youth drug use and had compiled years worth of data on student use trends. You won't know what you can find until you ask around.

Regional data are important for several programming reasons. First, it's important to know whether patterns you see locally are really just local problems. They may be much bigger, a reflection of state or national trends. You also want to know whether other areas of your state are sharing the problems you have found locally. Tap into their network to see what they have done that either did or did not work. Most important, depending on what the regional problem is, a school-based intervention may not be the best approach.

> **EXAMPLE:** A rural area in a northeastern state was showing consistently higher rates of crack cocaine use and arrests than any other part of the state even though it was not within 60 miles of an urban area. No other rural areas in the state were showing this trend. Something very specific to this region resulted in increased cocaine problems—but what? This regional trend was difficult to explain until someone figured out that it was related to access to one of the great lakes and the transportation of cocaine into the state through that county. This finding resulted in a law-enforcement-based intervention, and they were successful in making their area an undesirable place to get caught with cocaine on a boat. In this case, a school-based intervention would not have been effective.

Local Data

There are many sources of local data to which you may have immediate access. In most cases, the sources will provide you with only numbers, not names of students. Depending on the problem you have identified and the programming you will be developing, try some of these data sources:

Local Law Enforcement. Local departments will have statistics on DUI and DWI, statistics on types of crimes committed and in which neighborhoods, by which gender and age-groups. Often they can separate out youthful offenders or drug-related crimes.

Public Health Officials/Department of Health. All public health information will be here—data on incidence of disease; hospital admissions; acute hospital discharges; alcohol, tobacco, and drug illnesses and deaths; and substance abuse problems in newborns.

Department of Social Services. Every county has one. It has information on foster care, rates of child abuse, child abuse and neglect due to substance abuse issues, low-income families, poverty, unemployment, and often data on teen pregnancy and mental health. This is great information if you are writing a grant.

Town Planner. Local census data are often found here. Census data include information on single-parent homes, local demographics, housing starts, and population distribution statistics by age, race, and gender. This is another very good source of information if you are writing competitive grants.

Hospitals. In addition to birth and death statistics and incidence of disease mentioned above, hospitals keep emergency room data that can provide insight into overdose and other youth health crises.

Probation. Probation offices often have lots of youth data, including ages of youth on probation, reasons why youth are on probation, types of crimes, and whether the court recommended substance abuse intervention services.

School Records. To make data collection easy, many schools now keep discipline data (age, gender, grade, infraction date) on easy-to-use software (e.g., SchoolMaster, MacSchool, WinSchool). This is a great place to start with data collection, but don't stop here. Also collect data on absenteeism/attendance, suspensions/expulsions, and dropout rates. You may also learn a lot by talking with the school nurse.

Old Grants. How about old grants? These often contain summary data because the grantwriter before you had to do the data research. Even if the existing data you find are old, they may still be relevant as baseline or comparison data.

State and Local Alcohol Beverage Control Agencies. These agencies will have data on active liquor licenses. This information helps if you're planning a community intervention that targets illegal alcohol availability or sales.

National Institute of Alcohol Abuse and Alcoholism (NIAAA). This group has an Alcohol Epidemiologic Data System through which it maintains data on alcohol consumption for every state.

National Highway Traffic Safety Administration Fatal Accident Reporting System. This system tracks alcohol-related traffic fatalities. A reduction in alcohol-related traffic fatalities may be an indicator of program effectiveness.

SAMHSA's Uniform Facility Data Set. This tracks admissions to all treatment facilities.

Other Archival Data. Literally, what's in the archives? Has a needs assessment, health behavior survey, community survey, or opinion survey been conducted in the last 10 years? It may have been done by a community agency, school, hospital, local college, or just about any other group.

> **EXAMPLE:** A school group was searching for baseline data on student substance use. A parent on the committee remembered a project her son had done 3 or 4 years prior, in cooperation with the local newspaper, while working toward his rank of Eagle Scout (which he successfully earned). They had tabulated and published a rough student survey of drug use behaviors and attitudes. This group was able to use some of this information as baseline data.

▶ Access to Data

It's important to establish a real relationship with the people from whom you are receiving data. Know who collects the data from each agency/organization, learn their names, and for local resources, drive out to meet them. It will be a struggle to collect the data without a genuine relationship with the persons at the other end.

When you go to meet them for the first time, some of the information you will want to share with them or ask about will include the following:

▶ Share your reason for needing these data. You may want to give them a short statement about the purpose and design of your plan for program development and for assessing program effectiveness.

▶ Share a timeline for data collection and why you have established a monthly, quarterly, or yearly data collection plan.

▶ Ask for suggestions on how to work together to make this data collection-exchange as painless and nondisruptive as possible.

▶ Are there any official procedures for the release of the data? The procedure isn't always as easy as walking in and asking for the data. Some agencies or government offices have specific procedures that must be followed for release of data. Computer systems and reporting systems are also different. Some cases may involve laws regarding the release of data. Find out what you need to do to access the data, with whom you need to speak or from whom you need to get permission, and whether or not you need to submit an application.

▶ Really talk with those persons and remember to thank them. After all, they are saving you a huge amount of work.

Establishing a genuine dialogue with people who collect and control the data can even lead to their making changes in their data collection efforts to better meet your needs. One school found, after meeting with the local probation office, a way to change data collection that more clearly reflected the information the school needed and simplified the monthly reporting process for the probation office as well.

Student Surveys ◄

During the past 15 to 20 years, much controversy has surrounded the reliability and validity of student self-administered surveys. Student surveys are used widely because they're easy to administer, they're inexpensive, and schools can often tailor them to measure very specific needs or behaviors that are of local concern. Student surveys do have a place in program evaluation (Thomas, 1999).

It is now more necessary than ever to conduct student surveys to determine exposure to violence, attitudes, what drugs students are using, at what age they begin, and what they think about safety issues and drug use (see Resource R for information on student drug surveys). Many people are opposed to student surveys, citing the following reasons:

"Kids don't take them seriously, and the results won't be valid." Student substance abuse and violence surveys have become very serious business. Most of the better instruments now have validity safeguards ("lie scales") built in to ensure accuracy. These often work by asking similar questions in different ways. When run through the computer scoring process, the surveys that have inconsistent answering patterns are thrown out, as are surveys that are incomplete. This practice ensures a more accurate measure of student experience and attitude.

Some students habitually underreport their involvement with drugs and violence; some students overreport their involvement. If the **sample** size is large enough, these scores will, in effect, cancel each other out. The results *are* valid.

"We don't need that kind of information becoming public." Reputable survey providers never release survey results with your school's name attached. Generally the results are released to one administrator who then can choose any number of options for the public release of these data. Most often the data are grouped or synthesized to highlight selected problems, to show progress, or to identify areas where the district is doing better than state and national norms. Data can be presented in this way at community forums because parents and students are often quite interested in the survey results. It is a good idea to have a single media contact person and to prepare

written material for reporters to ensure accuracy of data and data interpretation (see Chapter 11 for a discussion of how to work more effectively with the media).

"Parental consent is too much of a nightmare." Because most student surveys don't track individual students and are unable to report results of specific students, active parental consent is generally not needed. It is always a good idea to inform parents that the survey will take place, allow them to preview the survey, provide the option of parents choosing to not allow their children to participate, and let students know that they also have the right to choose to not participate (see the information on the Protection of Pupil Rights Act [PPRA] in Chapter 6; PPRA, 1978).

"It's a violation of a student's right to privacy." Technically, it's not. Because no identifying information is being asked, privacy is not being violated. Participation in a survey is voluntary; students are generally allowed to opt out if they have strong feelings about it. Maintaining anonymity is key. For program planning purposes, a school simply needs to know what is happening, at what age, and by which group or gender. It is not necessary to know "who," and that should never be asked (review the Protection of Pupil Rights Amendment in Chapter 6).

⮞ Existing Services

Knowing what programs and services already exist will keep you from duplicating services. You may also find good programming that could benefit from some review and assessment. Data collection requires a thorough investigation of what services are already in place. This is called *assessment of program implementation and availability.* Program implementation and availability data you will want to collect may include the following:

Curriculum

Find out what prevention curriculum is being used in K-6, what resources are being used in junior high and high school health classes, and what pieces of curriculum integration exist, if any. Curriculum integration will generally be at the 7-12 grade level. Start by asking administrators about teacher training and materials. The Safe and Drug Free Schools Grants from previous years may also reflect curriculum, training, and materials purchased. Plan on talking briefly at a faculty meeting and talking with or surveying classroom teachers to determine exactly what they are doing in their classrooms. From your review of student behavioral data, can you tell whether existing programming is targeted at the right ages? Does it cover appropriate content? (See the "Sample Teacher Survey of Curriculum Content: Violence Prevention" in Resource S and the "Sample Teacher Survey of Curriculum Content: Substance Abuse Prevention" in Resource T.)

Materials

Browse through the school's libraries and see what kind of substance abuse and violence information is available to students at all grade levels. Are materials current? Are they accurate? Ask the librarians which books and periodicals get stolen; the answer may indicate what the students are most interested in.

Agency Services

Often many agency services are in place in schools. Again, begin with the building administrator and ask about service contracts, how they were selected, and what specific services are being provided. If possible, get copies of materials that agencies are using in classrooms.

Service Availability

Find out whether the school has special services such as crisis counselors or drug counselors, and explore the ease of access to them and the use of their services. Most keep their own version of a service log, which may yield some useful data.

Policy

When was the district policy on substance abuse or violence last revised? Does it still meet the needs of the students? Does it include incentives for non-use and clear sanctions for policy violations? Is it enforced consistently in all buildings and by all administrators? How well publicized is it? The school policy is the foundation of all program development. If you think you may need to do some work on the school policy, refer to resources specifically designed to guide you through that process (see Burk, 1998).

Objective Data Versus Subjective Information

The Principles of Effectiveness (U.S. Department of Education, 1998b) require that we use objective data to determine the needs of our population. It's very easy to confuse objective data and subjective information. **Objective data** are based on what can be observed and *measured*. Measurement is key. **Subjective information** includes impressions, judgments, opinions, as well as our interpretation of the facts. This interpretation can be distorted by personal feelings, experiences, or prejudices.

Examples of objective data are census data; law enforcement and crime statistics; health data such as disease, accident, and pregnancy rates; and school-based discipline data. Sources of subjective information include opinion surveys, press/media reports, group discussions, and anecdotes.

To make this discussion even more confusing, some subjective information can be proved accurate with objective data and measurement. For instance, not all media/press reports are subjective; many cite objective data. Opinion surveys may reflect general beliefs about certain behavior rates. Although they may be inaccurate when compared with objective sources of those data, the fact that 80% of those surveyed believe a problem exists is an objective fact.

A good example is the current perception of violence. Most people will tell you that crime and youth violence are increasing. As "proof" they will cite media reports of violent incidents around the country and their belief that things are getting worse. This information is actually all subjective and not based on fact. If we look at objective data on crime and youth violence, we see that school expulsions for weapons are down 32% and that youth-related violence in general is down 50%. What we believe (subjective) is sometimes different from the facts (objective). Programming decisions need to be based on objective data, the facts.

Often the words *quantitative* and *qualitative* are used to differentiate between objective and subjective information. **Quantitative** data are objective counts, rates, measurements, and statistics. These types of data are generally obtained through the use of behavioral surveys, observational checklists, and major data sets of state or national trends. Quantitative data are objective data.

Qualitative data are subjective. They are obtained through the use of interviews, focus groups, surveys of perceived problems, meeting minutes or correspondence, and even historical documents. This information is important, but it is not objective.

You will benefit most by using a combination of methods to collect the most complete information possible. For example, a student use survey will tell you what percentage of your students are smoking tobacco and at what age they are starting. This is only one piece of the tobacco use problem. Student focus groups or key informant interviews will provide you with additional information that will be crucial to program development, such as where students are getting tobacco products (vending machines, friends, parents, gas stations). A program to eliminate tobacco vending machines in your town will be very different from a program of parent education or enforcement of laws regarding sales to minors.

▣ Data Review and Summary

Once you've collected these data, you'll want to spend a chunk of time just looking at them, sifting through them all. As was stated before, it's more important to identify overall patterns than it is to notice specific numbers. Use the "Data Summary Log" in Resource U as you review the data. You should also review data in a group so that different perspectives can be heard. Here are some questions you might want to ask:

▶ What strengths does our school-community have? Are we taking advantage of these?

▶ Is our school-community growing, stable, or shrinking?

▶ Is the percentage of youth in our general population increasing, decreasing, or remaining stable? Will current programming be sensitive to potential changes in population size?

▶ Were the data gathered from a **random sample** of the population? Do they include a representative mix of gender, race, and age, or are gaps apparent in the data?

▶ At what age does tobacco use begin? Do we have our tobacco prevention program in the right grades?

▶ At what age does alcohol use begin? Do we start our alcohol prevention program at the right age?

▶ At what age does the use of illegal drugs begin? Do we begin drug prevention at the right time?

▶ At what age does bullying or harassment begin? Are our violence prevention programs starting early enough?

▶ What drugs are our students involved with, and at what rate are they using these drugs?

▶ What are student attitudes about drug use?

▶ What are the causes of youth emergency room visits?

▶ What are the most common crimes being committed by school-age youth? Are they happening on or off campus?

▶ At what age does violent or criminal behavior start?

▶ Does our community have higher than average incidents of any diseases, disorders, or other health conditions?

▶ What percentage of our school population receives reduced-cost lunch? What is the percentage of single-parent homes?

▶ Which gender is more involved with different incidents? Is our current programming targeted to this population?

▶ Do any numbers seem to covary? (e.g., With an increase in truancy, does vandalism increase or decrease? As age increases, does substance abuse increase or decrease?)

▶ How do these data compare with similar local, state, and national data?

▶ How have these data changed over time?

▶ How do the changes in these data compare with changes in similar regional, state, or national data?

To ensure that your substance abuse and violence prevention programming is targeted at the right age, it is most important to know at what age precursors to violent behaviors and drug use begin. Successful prevention programming needs to be in place before the behavior you want to prevent begins. In fact, that is the very definition of prevention.

▣ Important Things to Keep in Mind

1. *What is the problem, and at what age does it begin?* This information enables you to target programming for optimal success. For example, if you find a sharp increase in tobacco use between fourth and fifth grade, then your tobacco prevention program would be best implemented before fourth grade or before the behavior to be prevented has begun.

2. *What evidence do you notice that some data vary along with other data?* If substance use changes with age, then you may want to look more closely at those students to see whether you can identify probable causes for this possible connection. Target your programs to those causes.

3. *Are the programs you're currently providing supported by the data you've collected?* Are you spending 50% of your program funds on a violence prevention program but your data show that only one fight and no other campus violence occurred last year? To determine whether the spending matches the data:

a. Determine whether this was a significant violence decrease during the past 3 to 5 years. If so, then you have an excellent violence prevention program.

b. Are these data actually showing an increase in violence during the past 3 to 5 years? Then compare them with regional, state, and national data to see whether your increase was more or less than the national or state trend. If your increase was less than the regional, state, or national increase, then you may still be able to conclude that you have an effective violence prevention program.

c. Is this the same rate of violence you've had for the past 3 to 5 years (rate = incidence per capita student population)? If the rate is the same, then your violence prevention program appears to be having no impact, or perhaps the problem was so small to begin with that you didn't need the violence prevention program in the first place.

4. *Are there any gaps in service?* Do the data show an abundance of problem behaviors beginning at age 12 and almost no prevention programming in place before that? Have you identified some significant tobacco use problems but have no tobacco prevention programs in place and inconsistent tobacco policy enforcement?

5. *Are there any surprises?* Do you have significantly fewer DWI arrests when compared with regional, state, or national data? Is that the result of a stellar drinking-driving prevention program or a result of understaffed local law enforcement?

> **EXAMPLE:** One school was surprised when administrators found that the rate of female cigar smoking at their school was nearly 10 times higher than at other local schools. They narrowed this down to a celebration ritual of their female athletes. Targeted programming to that specific population reduced the rate of female cigar smoking.

> **EXAMPLE:** After reviewing similar data, another school found the expected levels of alcohol use across age and gender, but a surprisingly high percentage of the girls were riding as passengers in cars with intoxicated drivers. After conducting student focus groups to understand these data, school personnel discovered that girls were letting intoxicated boyfriends take them home from parties. They instituted assertiveness training for female students beginning 2 years before they began seeing this behavior. Subsequent data collections showed that this strategy was effective in reducing the incidence of girls riding as passengers with drunk drivers.

Two Warnings!

Warning 1

Once you isolate, define, and begin collecting data on specific behaviors, you may notice that for the first year all your numbers increase—even if you are doing effective programming! This does not necessarily indicate an increase in the actual incidence of behaviors. This may simply mean that observation and reporting procedures have improved. Many schools observed this phenomenon in the mid-1980s when suicide prevention programs were implemented. Data suggested a significant increase in suicidal students when, in fact, school employees, after training, were simply much better at making identifications and referrals. Their data leveled off, as will yours.

EXAMPLE: In one school, incidents of verbal harassment showed a significant increase during the same year a new violence prevention program was implemented. Interviews with teachers indicated that over the summer they had received specific training on referral of this particular problem. In the past, they would have handled it themselves in the classroom, but now they were required to send all students in violation of this policy to the office. Focus groups with students also supported the change in procedure for how incidents of verbal harassment were handled. From these numbers, we could not conclude that an increase in the incidence of verbal harassment had occurred; we could only conclude that an increase in referrals for verbal harassment had occurred.

Warning 2

Remember that no matter what program you have in place, increases in risk behaviors between the fourth and ninth grades will most likely occur. At those grade levels, the goal of prevention programming is not to reduce overall rates but to reduce the rate of increase.

◖ Second Thoughts

▶ Conduct a thorough collection of baseline data; this will result in accurately targeted prevention programs.

▶ Use national, state, regional, and local data for comparison.

▶ Collect data on existing programs, staffing, and materials.

▶ Make sure data reflect the entire school population or the entire community.

▶ Focus on the facts, the things that can be measured; use objective data rather than subjective information.

▶ Use student surveys to help you identify student attitudes and behaviors and at what age certain risk behaviors begin; this information will enable you to target programming accurately.

▶ Take your time in reviewing your data, identifying specific problems and populations in need of services, making sure current programs are in the right places, covering the right materials, and having the results you want. The extra care with your data will pay off in the end.

▶ Don't panic. All your numbers will most likely go up for the first year, reflecting better identification and reporting procedures, not necessarily an increase in student risk behaviors.

Self-Report Questionnaires and Focus Groups

6

Collecting Information From Students

A reasonable probability is the only certainty.
—Edgar Watson Howe, 1911

Student questionnaires and student focus groups are another way of collecting data from your population. They are two of the most popular techniques for collecting information from youth. The self-report questionnaire is used to measure rates and changes in attitudes and behaviors. When conducted properly, these tools can yield valuable information that will direct and correct program efforts. Both methods, however, are fraught with methodological land mines that can result in inaccurate information. Let's look at how to collect accurate information by using student questionnaires and student focus groups.

Self-Report Questionnaires

Probably the most used tool in local information collection efforts is the **self-report questionnaire.** It's the best way to collect specific data from targeted populations. It's easy, it's cheap, and the results are valuable. In most situations, the best choice is to use a nationally recognized student survey, some of which are listed in Resource R. These are valid, reliable, and normed on a huge national sample. When you purchase one of these surveys, they come with standardized administration directions, they are in an easy-to-complete format for your students, and when you are done you will receive a customized report of your school's results with excellent comparison data. If you have the money, purchase these services.

If you decide to create your own questionnaire because of a lack of funds or because of an interest in collecting information the standard questionnaires don't cover, know that assembling a questionnaire is serious business.

Some common factors govern all testing, factors that are easily overlooked when assembling your own questionnaire. We'll look at some fundamental features and construction rules for creating accurate self-report instruments.

This chapter may seem heavy, and the language may feel burdensome or intimidating. There is a reason for that. Creating a valid and reliable student survey can be burdensome and intimidating work. I want that to be very clear. You may want to look at the "Sample Student Risk Survey" in Resource V while we discuss these different survey features.

➤ Reliability

Reliability means consistency, stability. If you use any measuring tool, it should work in a similar way all the time. To be considered reliable, an odometer should give you the same result for every mile you drive. A self-report questionnaire should provide you with consistent and predictable results as well. If a self-report measurement of cigarette smoking always yields use rates that are similar to national statistics, then you can say it is reliable. If, however, this tool does not consistently produce those results, then it may not be a reliable measure of smoking behaviors.

Assuring Reliability in Your Questionnaire

There are five easy ways to check the reliability of the self-report questionnaire you develop.

Comparison

Comparison of your information with other similar regional, state, and national numbers is the first way to check reliability. If the information you are collecting looks nothing like regional, state, or national data, you may have a reliability problem with your instrument. Look closely at how your information was collected and the procedures that were used. Use one of the methods for testing reliability discussed below to determine whether your questionnaire is simply not reliable or whether your population really does have differences in behavior and attitude that cause it to look different from regional, state, or national data.

Multiple Scores Reliability

Think about how subjective sports like gymnastics or diving are scored: Multiple judges score the same observed behavior or performance. If the difference between the scores is slight, then this method is reliable. For school substance abuse and violence programs, determining reliability with multiple scores means collecting the same data from several different places. If the results you get from your questionnaire closely match other sources of information, then your questionnaire may be a reliable measure of this particular attitude or behavior.

Retest Reliability

Retest reliability is the most obvious method for determining reliability, by repeating the identical questionnaire on a second occasion without any intervening program and then comparing the scores. An instrument with high reliability will yield consistent results/scores when the same individual takes a **retest** (with an identical questionnaire or questionnaire of equivalent items) or under other variable exam conditions. If an individual result shows support for metal detectors on Monday and no support for them on Thursday, then very little confidence can be placed in the reliability of the questionnaire results.

Alternate Form Reliability

With *retest reliability,* you run into the problem of individuals remembering how they answered the questionnaire the first time around. With **alternate form reliability,** you avoid the problem of memory. This method involves using two comparable forms of the questionnaire: "Form A" and "Form B." The two forms should be as close to identical as possible without actually being the same. They should ask the same questions in different ways. The correlations between the scores on both versions should be close in order to show a high level of reliability. If you plan on using your self-report questionnaire often as a way to measure changes in student attitudes and behaviors from year to year, you may want to develop an alternate form to reduce the problems of memory.

Split-Half Reliability

Split-half reliability is easy because it involves a single administration of a single questionnaire. Afterward the items on the questionnaire are separated, or "split," making two comparable halves such as odd and even. The resulting two halves are scored as two separate tests, and the results are compared. The closer the results, the higher the reliability of the questionnaire.

Error variance can affect the accuracy of your survey results. Sometimes differences in results are found from one testing session to another or between students in different classrooms. When the conditions under which students complete the questionnaire (or any test) change the results, then there is said to be **error variance.** This has nothing to do with the actual content of your questionnaire. Error variance is caused by external factors, including time of day, temperature, sudden noises, distractions, illness, fatigue, and emotional state. Certain questionnaires will also have error variance that results from lack of standardized administration procedures. These procedures include differences in how the questionnaire was explained to the students and errors in scoring. Controlling the conditions under which the questionnaires are administered will reduce the error variance and increase the accuracy of the information you collect. The higher the reliability of the questionnaire, the less susceptible the results will be to daily changes in conditions. Additional non-program-related experiences may also affect questionnaire results, such as a change in grade levels, schedules, or teachers. Progressive developmental changes in students should also be considered. Children grow up and grow out of some attitudes and behaviors without any intervention at all, just time.

▣ Validity

Does the questionnaire actually measure what it claims to measure? Are you successful in measuring the identified variable of smoking behavior, or is the instrument actually a measure of fear of punishment or rule compliance? Whether or not a questionnaire measures what you want it to measure is called its **validity.**

> **EXAMPLE:** A semirural school district hired a local professional to assess the rates of different kinds of violence throughout the district. To the faculty's complete surprise, the results suggested extremely high rates of firearm violence, more than 10 times higher than state and national averages. They conducted focus groups with students in an effort to understand better why so many of them were involved with guns. They learned that many of their students were involved with hunting activities. The questions on the survey were not sensitive to sporting and recreational use of firearms. In this community, this survey was not a valid measure of firearm violence because it did not measure what it was claimed to measure.

If you are developing a self-report questionnaire to measure student attitudes toward substance abuse or violent behavior, be sure the questions you ask actually measure a student's attitudes or behaviors. This sounds simpler than it actually is. It may seem that the best way to determine student use behaviors would be to ask students about how often and how much they use. Sometimes this works well; other times their responses may not be completely honest or accurate. What you may actually learn from your questionnaire is what students want you to believe, not what is actually true.

Ensuring Validity in Your Questionnaire

As with the concept of reliability, there are a few ways to ensure a higher level of validity in your self-report questionnaire.

Judging

Judging is exactly what it sounds like: selecting "judges" to review all the questions in your draft questionnaire. This is the systematic examination of questions to determine whether they cover a representative sample of behaviors, skills, attitudes, or knowledge. Clearly define exactly what information you want to collect. Have the judges rate each item on whether they believe it will succeed at measuring what you are trying to measure. Use the items that your judges agreed were the best, and eliminate the items about which they disagreed. Enlist the help of your judges to rewrite items as well.

When selecting judges, include not only subject area experts but also members of the proposed audience—students. How students interpret questionnaire items is critical to collecting accurate information.

Criteria Referencing

Criteria referencing is done once you have clearly defined exactly what you hope your self-report instrument will tell you. You identify an independent, external "criterion" that will measure the same thing. Criterion information that is the most useful for determining the effectiveness of school-based prevention programs for students includes school grades, truancy records, police reports, and school policy violations. If your questionnaire shows that student substance use rates and incidents of violence are decreasing, then you would expect to see improvement in the criterion information, such as a decrease in policy violations. You want the numbers from your questionnaire and your criterion information to correlate.

If you develop a questionnaire on risk and protective factors for use in Grades 4 through 6 and then compare those scores with the rates of risk behaviors a few years later, you are using later risk behavior as your *validation data*. If the results of your questionnaire correspond closely with these validation data, then your questionnaire can be said to have a high level of **predictive validity.** That means it is a useful tool for predicting later student attitudes and behaviors.

If you find, through comparison with these criterion data, that your self-report questionnaire is not a good tool for what you're trying to measure, then you will need to redesign the instrument.

However you decide to determine the validity of your instrument, remember to (a) consult with subject matter experts when selecting items for your survey, (b) ensure that items are appropriate for and representative of your population's age, gender, culture, and learning styles, and (c) include student judges if this tool will be used with students.

Improving Reliability and Validity Through Construction

Keep in mind a few other things as you construct your self-report questionnaire. Simple things like format, length, administration, and interpretation of results are crucial for achieving higher levels of reliability and validity.

Format and Length

The format and number of items on your questionnaire can affect both its reliability and validity. Asking a single question will obviously not give you as much information or as accurate a picture as asking 10 questions. Take care, however, to keep in mind your audience, their attention span, reading level, and any special needs for testing that they may have. Keep length reasonable. Be prepared to produce your questionnaire in larger print, on colored or flecked paper, and in foreign languages as determined by the needs of your population.

Standardization

Standardization simply refers to uniformity of procedures for administering and scoring the instrument. The more standardized the procedures for administration, the greater the reliability you'll have in your results. Consider developing detailed written directions, exact duplicated materials for all test takers, oral instructions that are read from a script, preliminary demonstrations on how to use the answer forms if relevant, and specific rules for how to handle questions. Pay attention to all the details you reasonably can in order to maximize your reliability.

Norms

Most self-report instruments have no standards of "pass" or "fail." Most scores are interpreted by comparison with other scores. The "average" rates of certain behaviors would be the **norms**. State and national statistics are your best source of data for norms. As we saw in Chapter 5, **raw scores** are fairly meaningless without comparison data or something to measure them against.

With state and national norms, you can determine an individual's or group's position in relation to this normative sample. If your students average a score of 9 on a self-report inventory of alcohol use, it means little without something to compare it to. What does 9 mean? Is that high or low? If the average student (norm) scores a 14, and if students with scores above 20 have higher rates of criminal behaviors and referral to drug rehabilitation centers, then a score of 9 becomes more understandable. Remember that a norm is not the ideal or most desirable score; it is simply the average score for a given population.

Threats to Validity

Fake Good Responses

Self-report questionnaires are especially subject to faking answers. Despite how carefully you design each item, most often these instruments have one answer or an answer pattern that is recognizable as more acceptable or "correct" than others. On such tests, respondents may become motivated to *fake good responses* to appear better or more acceptable. Wouldn't you? A desired impression can be created this way and has been shown in plentiful research examples. Many people are not willing to share what they consider to be personal information. Some are not willing to admit to possible self-limitations, and others simply want to please the examiner. Fake good responses often result in inconsistent answering patterns, so a professional survey (see Resource R) can identify these questionnaires and throw them out. With a homemade questionnaire, you need to hope that the number of students who overreport certain behaviors will be matched by the number of students who underreport and so cancel each other out.

Situational Specificity

Behavior, as well as values and attitudes, can be *situationally specific*. This means that behaviors, attitudes, and values are not fixed and consistent across all situations. The students responding honestly to your questionnaire during English class may produce quite different answers if they were to take it home over the weekend or to take it while talking with peers during lunch. The people and situations surrounding students may change what they believe, their attitudes and values, and even their perceptions of their own behavior. This is a good reason for administering your questionnaire in a controlled environment.

Maturational Effects

Observed changes identified with your questionnaire from year to year may simply be caused by students growing up and out of certain behaviors or into others. Some oppositional behavior naturally drops off as students age. Substance use behaviors typically increase as students age. These examples are *maturational effects*.

Good Years and Bad Years

If your questionnaire results show unusually high rates of certain behaviors, it is likely that readministration at a later date will show rates that more closely conform to state or national norms. Most school communities do not show sustained levels of problematic behaviors. Schools and neighborhoods have *good years and bad years*.

Diagnostic Instruments

Resist the urge to design *diagnostic instruments*—questionnaires to diagnose alcoholism and other addictions, for example. They are difficult to validate, and that type of clinical judgment requires the skills of someone trained in differential diagnosis. Your self-report survey would be best used to identify rates of risk behaviors, attitudes, values, and perceived resources.

Anonymity

It will never be necessary to have student names attached to the information you collect. In fact, doing so is a huge liability. Because of the sensitive nature of the information being collected, you want to assure students and their parents that responses will remain anonymous. There is safety in anonymity. All you need for program planning is information that shows group trends you can separate by age, gender, or maybe socioeconomic or educational group.

You may have some involved adults who think it is important to connect sensitive information about drug use, drug dealing, and violent or criminal acts to specific students. Their argument will be that if the highest risk students can be identified, then we can get them help earlier. This is true; however, a survey of student behaviors and attitudes will yield the most accurate results if it is kept anonymous. A survey is not the appropriate place to conduct intervention activities.

Sometimes trying to create your own survey instrument is more time-consuming and expensive than you had planned. Quite a few valid and reliable instruments are already available to schools and communities. You may now be thinking that it is generally worth the expense to use one of these instruments. You are now a more informed consumer.

▶ Focus Groups

A **focus group** is a structured group interview. Generally this is a small group with 8 to 10 participants. They share their opinions, perceptions, and attitudes on a particular topic. Student focus groups have been used to collect information on student perceptions of school prevention efforts, advice on new directions, problems with teacher-student relationships, safety issues, administrative responsiveness to problems, and much more. This is a unique and often very effective method for hearing the students' perspective.

Running Focus Groups

Running focus groups does have potential problems. By paying attention to a few more details, you will increase the validity of the information you are able to collect by using this technique.

Group Selection

Recruit widely so that the group represents all age, race, gender, and clique differences. You may have to run more than one focus group on the same topic to ensure that all segments of your student body have a chance to be heard.

Make sure the group has no "one-of-a-kinds"—that is, single students of a particular race, gender, age, or clique. They may be reluctant to talk if they are not supported by another member of their subgroup. This inclusion requires that someone familiar with the student body be involved in the recruitment and selection of participating students. This person might be the student government adviser, assistant principal, school nurse, guidance counselor, or any other adult who interacts with a large percentage of the student body on a regular basis.

Room Selection/Environment

Select a room that is not too large, that is private, and that will have no interruptions. Establish a *safe environment* for disclosure of honest opinions. This includes more than just finding a quiet room that will have no interruptions. It requires that care be taken in selecting the adults who will be leading the group. For example, students may be more likely to share honestly with a guidance counselor than with the building principal. Having students involved with the selection of adult facilitators will maximize your success.

Scripted Questions

Develop a clear set of questions to guide the group discussion. Use the same questions with each group.

Hearing From Everyone

Elicit responses from all students. Protect unpopular, different, or minority opinions. Remember that it was difficult for the student to share.

Facilitator Neutrality

Do not show your opinion or provide responses to shared information. Revealing these will inadvertently change the nature of what is shared or the direction of the conversation. When collecting information from students in a focus group format, biasing or slowing the data collection through *adultism* can skew your information. Don't reinterpret what is said, and don't reword what is said when recording. When working with any population of a specific race or cultural background, make sure the person collecting the data is relatable to this group, "speaks their language," and can be neutral in the recording of the data.

Recording

Record everything that is shared in the words of the participants. Having a cofacilitator working as a recorder will help. You may also want to tape record the discussion.

Gratitude

Remember to thank students for their participation.

▶ Protection of Pupil Rights Amendment (PPRA)

The *Protection of Pupil Rights Amendment (PPRA)* was first introduced in Congress in 1978 as the Hatch Amendment to the Family Educational Rights and Privacy Act (FERPA). PPRA applies to all programs receiving funds from the U.S. Department of Education (ED). This amendment is intended to protect the rights of both students and parents in two ways. First, schools are required to make instructional materials available to parents if those materials are to be used in connection with an ED-funded survey, analysis, or evaluation in which their children are to participate. Second, schools must obtain parental consent before minor students are required to participate in any ED-funded survey, analysis, or evaluation that reveals certain information.

Active parent consent is required for any survey, analysis, or evaluation that reveals information concerning the following:

▶ Political affiliations

▶ Mental and psychological problems potentially embarrassing to the student and her or his family

▶ Sex behaviors and attitudes

▶ Illegal, antisocial, self-incriminating, and demeaning behavior

▶ Critical appraisals of other individuals with whom respondents have close family ties

▶ Legally recognized privileged or analogous relationships (lawyers, physicians, ministers)

▶ Income (other than required by law to determine eligibility for participation in a program or for receiving financial assistance under such a program)

Because substance abuse and violent behaviors can be considered "illegal, antisocial, self-incriminating" behaviors, you may choose to obtain active parent consent even if the survey you are using is anonymous. Some schools simply provide a consent form to all parents at the beginning of the year, explaining that the school is involved with the evaluation of programs that may affect their children. Parents sign and return this one form, and the school has parental consent for the remainder of the school year. With **pas-**

sive parent consent, parents do not have to actively respond unless they do not want their child participating. (See the "Sample Active Parent Consent Form" in Resource W and the "Sample Passive Parent Consent Form" in Resource X.)

Second Thoughts ◄

▶ Make use of the many good, valid, and reliable self-report questionnaires that are available. Sometimes the extra cost is worth using something you know will give you accurate results.

▶ Use the recommended methods for improving reliability and validity if you choose to design your own self-report questionnaire.

▶ Consult with subject matter experts when selecting items for your questionnaire.

▶ Know your population so that your questionnaire is appropriate for, and representative of, your population's age, gender, culture, and learning style.

▶ Include student judges if this tool will be used with students.

▶ Resist the urge to design an instrument that attempts to diagnose alcoholism or other addictions.

▶ Understand that the process of creating an accurate questionnaire may take more than a year.

▶ Keep focus groups small. Select a cross section of students, and use a predetermined set of questions.

▶ Correct situations that could lead to information bias.

▶ Keep your collected student information anonymous. Do not identify sample groups with student names, ever. Be careful so that information cannot be connected to a specific student.

▶ Be aware of your school policy as it pertains to PPRA and parental consent for student participation in surveys.

7 Cost and Time Effectiveness

Some circumstantial evidence is very strong, as when you find a trout in the milk.

—Henry David Thoreau, *Miscellanies*

Now it's time to start assessing your work and your program. By looking carefully at the time and cost effectiveness of your work, you will be able to redirect personnel or funds so that you can be more efficient. Looking at time and cost effectiveness is one way to look at program implementation.

▶ Cost Effectiveness

Examining the **cost effectiveness** of your program is more than necessary and a good first step in program assessment. In this area of programming, the numbers are easy to collect, easy to interpret, and often easy to adjust and repair.

Determine Actual Costs

Begin by adding up the actual costs of running your program (see the "Cost Effectiveness Worksheet" in Resource Y).

Personnel

Add the cost of all salaries, benefits, and overtime expenses for all people involved in implementing this program. These people will include direct program staff, as well as any support staff. Additional support staff might include the full-time-equivalent clerical person, bus drivers, maintenance, substitutes, coaches, lifeguards, chaperon stipends, outside speakers, and trainers.

Materials

Materials include any books, videos, folders, paper products, pens and pencils, computer software, and any other office supplies purchased for and dedicated to this program. Materials might also include smaller equipment items. Some funders have a rule that anything costing more than $500 or $1000 is considered "equipment" and that anything below the amount is a "supply." It doesn't matter where your cutoff is, as long as all your program supplies and equipment get counted.

Equipment

Include the cost of desks, chairs, VCRs/TVs, computers, file cabinets, coffee pots, all equipment purchased by this program. If some materials are shared between different programs, then figure out the percentage of time the equipment is used by your program and use that percentage of the cost.

Purchased Services

Purchased services includes any expenditures on service contracts, telephone lines, repair contracts, equipment rentals (e.g., roller skates, video projection), hotel rooms, janitorial or transportation services, even tuition—any "service" that you purchase from a service provider.

Space

What does it cost to use the space where the program takes place? Are you paying rental or usage fees? Do you have to pay for retreat facilities? Are you paying for off-hours use of public facilities?

Miscellaneous

The miscellaneous category includes all expenses that aren't captured in the other categories—the cost of food, travel, any registration fees, memberships, and subscriptions. Remember to include the cost of hotel rooms, tolls, and parking.

Gross Program Cost

Add up the total from each of the above six categories. Count every last penny, every receipt for toll, every roll of masking tape, every pay stub, rent check, and equipment cost. This will yield a large number. This is your *gross program cost,* or actual program budget.

Unduplicated Participant Count

Determine how many students were directly involved with this program, taking care as always to be accurate. If you ran groups, how many students participated? If you provided counseling, how many students were counseled? How many students participated in your tutoring program—both as tutors and as tutees? Be careful not to use a duplicated count. Some state forms ask you to count units or hours of service. That is not an accurate count of the actual number of students involved. Count students accurately by making a list of names if you have to.

Estimated Cost per Participant

Divide the gross program cost by the total number of students. If Program A cost $21,500 and 30 students were involved, then you can estimate a **per student cost** of $717 dollars. If Program B cost $800 and 30 students were involved, then you can estimate a per student cost of approximately $27. You can conclude that Program B was more cost effective. You *cannot* say that Program B was more effective, just that it was less expensive per student to run.

What else do we know by looking at these numbers?

a. *Was the actual program budget "equipment heavy" in this first year?* Program A cost $717 per student. Will a significant reduction in program costs be seen during the next few years now that the equipment has been purchased?

b. *How does the cost per student for this type of program compare with that of other similar programs in your area?* You may want to make some calls to see whether any other local programs are keeping similar data you can use for comparison.

c. *Where can you easily cut or adjust expenses?* Review all program expenses, looking for places where you can further reduce costs. Can a local business or fraternal organization donate materials? Can you use volunteers rather than paid workers (paying stipends)? Can you get space donated, rather than pay rent or a fee for usage? Look closely at your numbers, and see what can be improved.

d. *How can you increase student involvement?* The total cost per student can be reduced not only by reducing expenses but also by increasing the number of students who participate. Is this feasible, given your staff and space limitations? If so, plan to increase your advertising and broaden your selection criteria.

Final program reports often allow for a budget narrative where you can share this information. Do not just share your gross program cost and total cost per student but also describe how the financial picture for this program will be different next year. Explain planned changes that will increase or reduce costs.

Time Effectiveness ◀

How much staff time is dedicated to implementing this program—100%? 50%? You may not really know until you start keeping deliberate records of how you spend your minutes, your **time effectiveness.** To keep track of your time, start by using the "Time Management Worksheet" (see Resource Z) or design your own written method for keeping track of how your time is spent. To use the "Time Management Worksheet," identify the different programs for which you will be measuring staff time distribution. Table 7.1 shows this worksheet as it would appear completed for 1 day.

Completing these computations for a single day will not give you an accurate picture of time distribution. Some programs only take place 1 day each week, a few days each month, or during a particular season or semester. Some days of the week may require more counseling than others, depending on events that occur. By collecting these types of data over the course of weeks or months, you will have a larger, and therefore more accurate, base of data. Remember that we also want to control for **sampling error.**

For the purposes of walking through the process once, we will be using the example in Table 7.1 of time distribution for 1 day. When you do this with your own program, you will be using data from several weeks, and your numbers will be much larger.

The "Time Management Worksheet" has you recording your time worked in "units," which represent quarter-hour segments of time. After completing the worksheet, compute the total minutes dedicated for each program by counting the number of units and multiplying by 15 (minutes) (see Table 7.2.)

Now take the total number of minutes for each program and divide it by the total number of minutes in that workday to determine the percentage of time being dedicated to each program (see Table 7.3). If you are using larger numbers that represent several weeks or months, you will do the same thing. Take the total number of minutes for each program and divide it by the total number of minutes for the week, month, or whatever period you are measuring. Remember that this is approximate, not exact. The accuracy is entirely dependent on the staff person's record keeping.

TABLE 7.1 Time Management Worksheet

Program A: _____Student Counseling_____   Program B: _____Student Support Groups_____

Program C: _____Peer Tutoring_____   Program D: _____Peer Leadership_____

Time	Activity	Program
7:00-7:15	Paperwork	C
7:15-7:30	Paperwork	C
7:30-7:45	Paperwork	C
7:45-8:00	Student	A
8:00-8:15	Student	A
8:15-8:30	Student	A
8:30-8:45	Student	A
8:45-9:00	Student	A
9:00-9:15	Student	A
9:15-9:30	Phone	D
9:30-9:45	Prep	B
9:45-10:00	Prep	B
10:00-10:15	Group	B
10:15-10:30	Group	B
10:30-10:45	Group	B
10:45-11:00	Phone	A
11:00-11:15	Phone	A
11:15-11:30	Charting	A
11:30-11:45	Charting	A
11:45-12:00	Lunch	
12:00-12:15	Lunch	
12:15-12:30	Phone	A
12:30-12:45	Phone	A
12:45-1:00	Group	B
1:00-1:15	Group	B
1:15-1:30	Group	B
1:30-1:45	Charting	B
1:45-2:00	Charting	A
2:00-2:15	Meeting	A
2:15-2:30	Meeting	A
2:30-2:45	Paperwork	A
2:45-3:00	Paperwork	C
3:00-3:15	Leave for home	

TABLE 7.2 Conversion of Units to Minutes

Program	Units		Total Minutes/Day
Program A	16 units	x 15	= 240 minutes/day
Program B	9 units	x 15	= 135 minutes/day
Program C	4 units	x 15	= 60 minutes/day
Program D	1 unit	x 15	= 15 minutes/day

TABLE 7.3 Percentage Time at Each Program

Total minutes at work today (minus lunch) = 450 minutes

Total minutes for Program A	240 minutes ÷ 450 minutes	53%
Total minutes for Program B	135 minutes ÷ 450 minutes	30%
Total minutes for Program C	60 minutes ÷ 450 minutes	13%
Total minutes for Program D	15 minutes ÷ 450 minutes	3%

By displaying the time spent on each program in percentages, we get an easy-to-understand picture of where each staff member is spending her or his time. Time distribution data will allow you to make accurate decisions about staff use, program direction, and training needs.

EXAMPLE: One school found, after collecting time use data like these, that the program director was spending over 50% of her time doing direct service to students who were in violation of the school drug and alcohol policy. On the basis of these data, guidance staff received training to perform some of the student assessment work, thus freeing the program director's time enough to write grants securing additional funds to hire a drug and alcohol counselor.

EXAMPLE: Another school found that staff were spending an inordinate amount of time on material development—computer work, specifically. As a result of these time use data, some staff received training on computer usage, graphic design, and other computer tools to make their work on the computer much more efficient.

Return always to your original data to determine needs and resulting program goals. If you determined that leadership and tutoring programs were the best program options for reducing your students' risk behaviors, and if your time distribution data indicate that your staff time priorities are not consistent with these program goals, then changes need to be made. You have just taken the first step, and an important one, in assessing your program's effectiveness.

▶ Second Thoughts

▶ The more data you have, the more accurate your numbers will be and the more relevant your conclusions can be.

▶ Cost effectiveness means taking a hard look at where the money in your program budget is spent and making improvements year to year so that your expenditures are in line with your program goals and objectives.

▶ Does your time distribution match with your program goals? This means if you hired a drug and alcohol counselor, then that person should be spending the majority of time doing drug and alcohol counseling. If you hired a peer leadership coordinator, then that person should be spending the majority of time coordinating peer leadership programs.

▶ Your numbers will be most accurate if record keeping is a daily habit rather than a monthly guesstimate.

Experimental Design

8

The Basics

The whole of science is nothing more than a refinement of everyday thinking.

—Albert Einstein, 1950,
Out of My Later Years

Having an experimental design allows you to assess your program's success through an orderly process of data collection and observation. This means looking systematically at your student data to see whether your program is making an impact.

You have already collected and analyzed your local data, you have identified problem areas, you have written your goals and objectives, and you have selected or written the program you believe will have the greatest impact. After implementing your program, your next step is to collect and compare outcome data with baseline data. How do things look? Were you successful in changing student attitudes or behaviors? If not, why not? And if you were successful, could you have been even *more* successful? These last two questions are the ones an experimental design will help us answer.

This portion of research is called *methods,* or "exactly how did you control for all those variables and draw accurate conclusions?" It won't be as difficult as you think. As you'll see, only after you control those variables will you be able to attribute changes in student behavior to the program you used and draw accurate conclusions (see Figure 8.1).

Technically, a **variable** is any behavior, attitude, or characteristic that can be measured. Height, weight, age, gender, and grade level are all variables. Behaviors like teasing, bullying, and quantity and frequency of cigarette smoking and alcohol use, and attitudes like perceived harm from use are also variables. It is necessary to identify exactly what variables you hope to change and then make sure you collect data specific to those variables. You identified your variables when you wrote your program objectives.

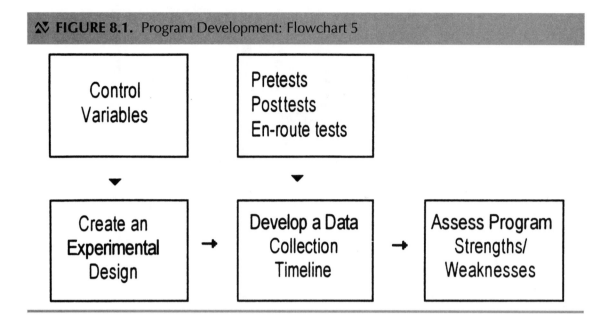

FIGURE 8.1. Program Development: Flowchart 5

Experimental Design

Don't be intimidated by the language. It is really just descriptive of how you are going to set up your data collection and provide program services. Your *experimental design* is a way of fine-tuning your program. How many groups? How many conditions? When will you be administering pre- and **posttests**? You want to be able to show outcome measures that indicate participants have changed as a result of their participation in your program. The key issue in setting up your experimental design is proving that preprogram and postprogram changes were the direct result of participation in your program and had nothing whatsoever to do with any other influence.

The many confounding factors, called **extraneous variables,** include mass media events (e.g., the shootings at Columbine High School), personal or family events (e.g., health changes, divorce/remarriage, moving, unemployment), and changes in the school experience (e.g., change in teachers, scheduling) that can sometimes lead to significant student behavior change. Your experimental design can even become an extraneous variable if data collection is not done properly. How do you separate out the effects of your program from the effects of these extraneous variables?

Data gathering design can be a huge factor in ruling out explanations for behavior changes other than the program itself. When and whom you measure is the key to your experimental design.

Sample Size

Sample size means how many people will be receiving the program. Your **sample** is the subset of the general population involved with your program.

Are there 82 individuals? 17 families? 42 classrooms? 8 schools? If your program is targeted to individuals, then you will be measuring individual behaviors as your outcome measure. If your program is targeted to families, then you will be using some criterion of family functioning as your outcome measure. If your program is targeted to school buildings, then you will be using building-wide change data as your outcome measure.

For your data to be the most valid, your sample size must be as large as possible. One reason is that individual cases or small groups do not make for good science. If you only measure a program's impact on two students, you will not get a valid picture of the program's effectiveness. If your group is small, it is far easier to attribute program outcomes to coincidence, rather than to the actual program. Even the most outstanding results can be blamed on chance if the sample size is small. This is called *sampling error*. The inaccuracies, or errors, in your results were caused by your small or nonrepresentative sample.

A second reason for starting with a large sample size is attrition. Inevitably students will drop out of your program or will move out of the school district. The larger your sample is to begin with, the better it will withstand this natural reduction in numbers.

Types of Measures

Pretests

Pretests are used to collect participant data before program implementation. These are your baseline data. It doesn't necessarily have to be a "test"; that's a bit of a misnomer. It can also be a "rate" or a "frequency" or any other type of preprogram measure. The pretest data you collect will be tied directly to the behavior change you expect this program will produce. If you believe that involvement in your program will reduce the frequency of verbal outbursts, then you must begin with a preprogram measure of the frequency of verbal outbursts. If you believe that involvement in your program will reduce the quantity and frequency of smoking behavior, then you must begin with a preprogram measure of the quantity and frequency of smoking behavior (see the "Sample Youth Participant Pretest" in Resource AA). You may want to get preprogram measures, rates, and data on some other related behaviors to see whether your program will have broader impact on them as well.

In most cases, you will want to collect both preprogram rates and frequencies of various behaviors, as well as more specific participant information, such as attitudes and beliefs. To collect specific participant information, you may want to design a brief survey instrument. Refer to Chapter 6 for how to do this.

En-Route Tests

En-route tests are measurements taken or administered during your program. Most often these are used as *process measures*, or measures of program implementation rather than effectiveness. Is the room comfortable? Is this the best time of day or the best day of the week? Should you include more or fewer activities? These tests are most appropriate for programs of long duration (see the "Sample En-Route Participant Feedback" in Resource L).

Immediate Posttests

Most often *immediate posttests* are administered immediately following a program. They should be the same as or very close to the pretest instrument used. This way, posttest data can be compared with pretest data to see the direction and magnitude of behavior change. These results can also be compared with posttest results from other programs. Again, *test* is a bit of a misnomer. This also includes the collection of rates and frequencies of other attitudes and behaviors.

Delayed Posttests

Delayed posttests are the real "proof" of program effectiveness. A delayed posttest measures long-term rather than short-term change in participant attitudes and behaviors. Because the most desirable outcomes from drug and violence prevention programs are long-term changes in behavior, this information is critical. Unfortunately, it is the most inconvenient to collect.

Program Design Strategies

Now you will design a system of data collection that allows you to compare the results of different programs or different versions of the same program. This is like a field test to see whether these techniques or this program content was as effective in changing the attitudes and behaviors of your students as you believed it would be.

One Group Pretest-Posttest Design

The simplest experimental design is the *one group pretest-posttest design*. This involves measuring your population, implementing the program, and remeasuring your population.

Measurement → Program → Measurement

This design is very common because it's easy, but there are many problems with the resulting data. First, how do you attribute measured changes to your program and not to some extraneous variable, like a mass media event? Second, how do you know whether the changes you observe are as good as or better than the changes in people who were in a different program or who received no program at all?

Control Group Design

You can significantly improve your data by employing a *control group design.* A **control group** is a sample of the same size and same characteristics (e.g., age, race, gender) as those who receive your program, only they don't get to participate in the program. The easiest way to create a control group is to split your original sample and randomly provide your program to half of them.

Measurement →   Program   → Measurement

Measurement → No Program (control group) → Measurement

Your resulting data will show (we hope!) that students who were in your program exhibit behavior changes that surpass those of students who were not in your program. If both groups have similar posttest data, then you will know that the program may not be effective as a method for changing student behavior.

Maturation of participants will naturally result in higher levels of certain risk behaviors, like substance abuse. This means it is likely that students who participate in a substance abuse prevention program will still show increases in substance use. This does not mean your program had harmful effects or caused increases in student drug use behaviors. By using a control group, you can show that all students in this age-group showed an increase in substance use behaviors but that the students in your program showed *less* of an increase than students who were not in your program.

Comparison Group Design

A third method, called *comparison group design,* involves separating an initial sample into two or more groups, providing them with different programs or different versions of the same program, and then comparing posttest data to see which program was the most effective.

Measurement → Program A → Measurement

Measurement → Program B → Measurement

For example, assume that your school has two different peer leadership programs. You want to determine whether one is more effective than the other. You would set them up as **comparison groups.** In this way, you will be able to identify which program was more effective in changing student behaviors. However, you won't know *why* one program worked better than the other. To determine this, you must carefully and systematically control different variables.

Controlling Variables

Variables are very difficult to control because they can occur both deliberately and accidentally. Consider the following example.

> **EXAMPLE:** A suburban school was running support groups for children of alcoholism in an effort to increase academic functioning. Group content included identifying good times and places to study, improving study skills, accessing tutors, and connecting some of the group participants with the district reading specialist. Each of the three groups had 10 students. Each group was facilitated by a different social worker using the same group curriculum. Posttests at 3-, 6-, and 12-month intervals indicated that two of the groups showed significant decay in acquired skills, whereas the third group continued functioning at a higher level without decay in acquired skills.

This is an excellent example of the effects of an unplanned variable. Something was different about the third group. It could be the personality of the group facilitator, the dynamics of the participant blend, something that was added to the curriculum, or the time or location of the group. To repeat the success of the third group, you must first isolate and identify the variables that caused the differences in participant outcome.

Controlling variables can be tricky because any given situation comprises hundreds of variables. To test a particular variable, it is important that everything possible be kept exactly the same between the two conditions (Program A and Program B) except for the one variable you are testing.

If you want to determine whether the program is more effective as a daily program over 3 weeks (Program/Condition A) or a weekly program over 3 months (Program/Condition B), you would pretest all students and collect other baseline measures of attitudes and behaviors, randomly assign the students to one of the two program conditions, and then implement both programs with exactly the same materials and activities—even in the same room, at same time of day, and with as many things as possible the same between the two conditions except that Program A meets daily for 3 weeks and Program B meets weekly over 3 months. As much as possible, the length of the program should be the only difference between the two conditions. Take immediate posttest measures and delayed posttest measures at predetermined intervals. Also consider en-route tests for feedback from students and the adult facilitators so that you know how each condition "feels" to participants.

Compare your data between the two treatment conditions. If you find that one program/condition showed greater behavior change over a longer duration (as determined from posttest data), then you have objective data to support conducting all programming in that delivery model. If you find no significant differences in outcome measures of behaviors, attitudes, or skills between the two program conditions, then you can base your programming decision on participant feedback, or process evaluation. If participants liked it better as a condensed program, then there is no reason not to do it that way in the future.

No matter which variable you seek to measure, the procedure will be the same. Control as many other variables as possible so that you're most likely to be measuring the one variable you are deliberately varying between groups. Other program variables, in addition to content, you may want to measure are gender of facilitators, gender mix of participants, time of day, length of session, length of program, ratio of activities to lecture, on or off school grounds, with or without parental involvement, and with or without booster sessions. This list can be endless.

You can take this design a step further either by adding different programs/conditions or by adding a control group.

Measurement → Program A → Measurement

Measurement → Program B → Measurement

Measurement → No program (control group) → Measurement

By adding a control group, you can show that both of these programs are "better than nothing." With the comparison groups, you can also compare them with each other. Once you establish that they are effective programs, you can deliberately change program design, implementation, or content and measure your results. Continue to compare your results with those of the other programs and see what changes lead to the best results.

Ideally you will eventually be able to prove that your program can produce similar positive results with a different participant population (e.g., males vs. females, different ethnicities) or that the positive effects can be achieved even with slight variations in the program or a change in program personnel. This is called establishing **external validity.**

Is change enduring? Delayed posttest measures are crucial for determining that. Posttest your group at planned intervals after the program is completed: 1 month, 3 months, 6 months, 1 year, 2 years, and even into the participants' next school if that's possible.

One major problem with delayed posttest is attrition. Students drop out, move, or graduate. They grow up, change their names, or leave town. It's sometimes very difficult to follow them. Having a large sample size that will withstand some attrition is important.

Measuring Community Change

What if you want to measure the effectiveness of a community-wide program, a media blitz of prevention messages, or information dissemination at parents' night? In what ways can you measure the effectiveness of these larger and less structured activities?

Quasi-Experimental Designs

How do you measure the effectiveness of distributing informational brochures at a community fair? The following methods are called **quasi-experimental designs** because they aren't as scientifically accurate as we would like, but they follow the general principles of the experimental designs just described and will produce usable results.

Nonequivalent Comparison Group

The *nonequivalent comparison group* is the same as control group design except that assignment to each group or condition is not random. You begin by selecting a community that is as similar as possible to yours, based on predetermined criteria such as socioeconomic status, size, and similar alcohol and tobacco policies and enforcement. Then you compare postprogram data between the two groups.

Measurement Community A ➜   Program   ➜ Measurement

Measurement Community B ➜ No Program ➜ Measurement

This is not the best method for determining the effectiveness of your program, because it is difficult to attribute posttest differences to the intervention of brochure distribution. There are simply too many possible confounding variables. The differences you see might be attributable to a concurrent prevention program, a media event, or even a price change in a product rather than the result of your program.

Time Series Design

In *time series design,* measurements of the population are taken for months or years before the program is actually implemented and then for months or years after the program has been in place. All data are plotted or graphed to identify trends or changes and whether they coincided with the program.

Measure ➜ Measure ➜ Measure ➜ Program ➜
Measure ➜ Measure ➜ Measure

When data are plotted over time, you hope to see a spike in the graph or a ripple in the data during the time when the program was in place. It's still difficult to conclude that your program caused the ripple in the data, because so many other things may have happened at the same time, coincidentally.

You will have a better chance of proving that your program was the cause of the behavior change if you introduce it at different times and in different places and it continues to coincide with ripples in your plotted data. You can also add support to causality, or show that your program actually was the cause of the change you have measured, by adding data from a comparison group (like a neighboring community) that has the same data collection schedule without the ripples in data seen in the community receiving the program.

Having an experimental design means you have an organized way to collect data and determine program effectiveness. It is not intimidating if you have followed all the steps of program development and assessment so far outlined. Identify your problem based on your data and then select and implement the program you think will best change student behaviors. Finally, re-collect your data to see whether you can draw any valid conclusions. If you can conclude from postprogram data that your program has had an impact—especially an enduring impact—then you have a program that people will want to hear about.

Second Thoughts

▶ You will be a step ahead if you design your data collection plans before any programming takes place.

▶ Your experimental design is developed to test or prove that "Program X can cause Behavior Change Y."

▶ The larger your sample size, the more valid your resulting data.

▶ Control groups are important for comparison purposes and accounting for extraneous variables. It's worth the time and effort to establish a control group.

▶ Delayed posttest measures are crucial for determining how enduring behavior change will be.

▶ Quasi-experimental designs, though not scientifically rigorous, can be used when measuring community change.

9 | Experimental Designs for Different Program Types

The plural of "anecdote" is not "evidence."
—Alan Leshner, President - NIDA

This chapter contains some generalized examples of assessment plans for different types of prevention programs. These are not specific enough to be used as written, but with a little work and the addition of data, details, and program definitions specific to your program, this is a place to take a shortcut.

Five program types are outlined: (a) student assistance programs (SAPs), (b) elementary prevention curricula, (c) after-school activities, (d) student support groups, and (e) student leadership programs. For each program type and program definition, ideas for data collection, goals and objectives (both process and outcome), and a description of an appropriate experimental design are provided to help you assess effectiveness.

These examples are solid experimental designs. They can be improved by adding more measurements or variables, by adding more comparison groups, and by using your local mathematics class, mathematics teacher, or friendly statistician to help with the numbers. Your creativity and imagination will only improve this process.

► Student Assistance Programs (SAPs)

SAP Program Definition

A *student assistance program (SAP)* is designed to identify students who are at risk and to provide intervention services, thereby lowering student rates of high-risk behaviors. It is believed that by identifying students who are at risk prior to their involvement with substance use and by providing them with a relevant intervention, later rates of substance abuse can be lowered.

Data Collection

Students are identified for SAP services on the basis of lowered academic performance, truancy, school attachment problems, association with negative peers, lack of self-control, impulsive behavior, poor social competencies, peer rejection, or other identified risk behaviors.

Objective data on these risk factors can be found in school academic records, school attendance records, teacher observation reports, school discipline records, guidance reports, school nurse records, and at local probation and law enforcement agencies.

Program Goal of an SAP

An SAP goal is to reduce the overall level of risk behaviors or a specified risk behavior within a specified population of students.

Objectives

Process Objectives

1. By (specify date), two full-time staff members will be dedicated to providing identification and intervention services to students in Grades 7 through 12.

2. By (specify date), 30 students will have received services from the SAP program.

Outcome Objectives

1. Truancy among 7th through 12th graders will decrease by 10% by (specify date).

2. Rates of on-campus substance use among 9th through 12th graders will decrease by 25% by (specify date).

Experimental Design

Our evaluation will use a comparison group design with pre-, en-route, immediate post-, and delayed postmeasures. The comparison group will be a school of similar size, demographics, socioeconomic status, and academic status. We may use a school within our own district that will not be implementing this program for another year.

Data on identified risk behaviors that we will collect prior to implementing the SAP program will also be collected at the comparison school. These data will be examined midyear (en-route), at the end of the school year (immediate post-), and in the fall of the next school year (delayed post-).

Data from the two locations will be compared for similarities, differences, and possible confounding variables. Confounding variables to be examined will include differences in record keeping between the two locations, differences in the enforcement of school policy, differences in the handling of disciplinary infractions between building administrators, and any school-specific events or traumas that might account for across-the-board changes in student behavior.

▶ Elementary Prevention Curriculum

Elementary Prevention Curriculum Definition

An *elementary prevention curriculum* is a series of lessons designed to increase knowledge and skill levels of participating students, thereby reducing later risk behaviors. It is believed that by implementing an elementary prevention curriculum, later rates of risk behaviors can be lowered.

Data Collection

Data collection for curriculum effectiveness will be done at grades beyond where the curriculum is implemented. If this is a substance use prevention curriculum, then all data related to substance use rates in later grades need to be collected. This often requires implementation of a regular schedule of student use surveys (see Resource R) every 2 or 3 years to monitor changes in use patterns. It is also important to measure at what age alcohol, tobacco, and drug use begin.

If this is a violence prevention curriculum, then all data specific to harassment, fighting, or other identified violent acts need to be collected. This may require monthly data summaries of school-related incidents to monitor changes. Determine at what age these incidents begin to ensure proper program placement.

Goal of Prevention Curriculum

An elementary prevention curriculum goal is to reduce the amount or frequency of drug use, delay age of first use, or increase the rate of abstinence within a specified population.

Objectives

Process Objectives

1. By (specify date), 100% of elementary teachers will have received training in this prevention curriculum.

2. By (specify date), 80% of classrooms will have implemented this prevention curriculum.

Outcome Objectives

1. Rates of tobacco use among 7th through 9th graders will decrease by 20% by (specify date).

2. Age of first use of alcohol will increase by 0.5 year by (specify date).

Experimental Design

Our evaluation will use a control group design with pre- and delayed postmeasures of alcohol, tobacco, and other drug use. The control group will be found within our own district and will be made up of students in Grades 1 through 6 who are not receiving this prevention curriculum in their elementary classrooms.

Data on tobacco, alcohol, and other drug use rates, as well as age of first use, will be collected in Grades 7 through 12 prior to implementing this curriculum. These data will be re-collected and examined at 2-year intervals; *when* the students receiving this curriculum enter into our testing sample will be noted.

Data from the two groups will be compared for similarities, differences, significant differences, and possible confounding variables. Confounding variables to be examined will include implementation of other prevention materials in classrooms and variations in teacher training.

After-School Activities

After-School Activities Definition

An *after-school activity* will include any school-sponsored activity that is ongoing (more than 8 weeks), that takes place between the hours of 3:00 p.m. and 6:00 p.m., and that is outside the current school athletic program. It is believed that by providing structured, ongoing activities for students during the period of 3:00 to 6:00 p.m., rates of crime and vandalism will be lowered in the community.

Data Collection

Data on current crime rates, ages of perpetrators, types of crimes, and locations of property crimes can be collected from local law enforcement, school discipline records, and the local probation department.

Goal of After-School Activities

By providing after-school activities, rates of property crimes will decrease.

Objectives

Process Objectives

1. By (specify date), two stipend positions will be created for staff to supervise after-school activities.

2. By (specify date), 25 students will be participating in after-school activities.

Outcome Objectives

1. Property crimes committed between 2:30 p.m. and 6:00 p.m. will decrease by 25% by (specify date).

2. Rate of campus vandalism will decrease by 40% by (specify date).

Experimental Design

Our evaluation will use a comparison group design with pre-, immediate post-, and delayed postmeasures. The comparison group will be a regional school of similar size, demographics, socioeconomic status, and academic status with similar rates of property crimes. We will use our county police in analyzing data to select the comparison community.

Data on property crimes on and off campus will be collected from both communities prior to implementing our after-school program. These data will be examined immediately following our program and then routinely at 3-month intervals to see whether they change in relation to program activities.

Data from the two locations will be compared for similarities, differences, and possible confounding variables. Confounding variables to be examined will include changes in police staffing or enforcement during the study period and other crime prevention initiatives taking place in either community.

Student Support Groups ◄

Student Support Groups Definition

A *student support group* is an ongoing group (6-10 weeks) of structured content intended to provide education, skill development, and support for students identified as being in need of such services. It is believed that by providing the intervention of student support groups for identified students, early problem behaviors and resulting consequences can be reduced.

Data Collection

Depending on the purpose of the support group, the data that are collected may differ. For example, if this support group is for students with poor social competency skills, then data collected will likely include self-report data on feelings of social comfort and observational data (teacher/parent feedback) on the students' ability to solve social problems, display empathy, and interact in a socially appropriate manner.

Measurement of consequence rates, such as after-school suspensions and disciplinary referrals, can be used for support groups designed to address more specific behavior problems such as anger management. Be as specific as possible in defining the purpose and goal of the group, and be as concrete and objective as possible in collecting pregroup data.

Goal of Student Support Groups

The goal of a student support group is to provide education, skill development, and support for students identified as being in need of such services. Participation in such a group will reduce future risk behaviors.

Objectives

Process Objectives

1. By (specify date), two guidance staff and four additional staff will be trained in the facilitation of student support groups.

2. By (specify date), two student support groups will be ongoing.

Outcome Objectives

1. Referrals for talking back and similar oppositional behaviors will decrease by 10% by (specify date).

2. Students involved in support groups will report a 25% increase in feelings of social comfort at the conclusion of group.

3. Students involved in the support group will have teacher/parent observational checklists that reflect a 25% improvement in the identified behavior by (specify date).

Experimental Design

Our evaluation will use a control group design with pre-, en-route, immediate post-, and delayed postmeasures. The control group will be made up of students referred for participation in the group who are randomly selected to not participate.

Data on identified social skills will be collected from our control and experimental groups through the use of self-report instruments. Data will also be collected through the use of teacher/parent observational checklists.

We will collect en-route process data to determine whether the support group facility is appropriate.

Delayed postmeasures will be collected from both the experimental and control groups through the use of self-report measures. Delayed postmeasures will also be collected through the use of teacher/parent observational checklists.

Data from the two groups will be compared for similarities, differences, significant differences, and possible confounding variables. Confounding variables to be examined will include any differences in data collection and any school-specific events or traumas that might account for across-the-board changes in student behaviors.

▶ Student Leadership Programs

Student Leadership Programs Definition

A *student leadership program* is any program that provides the opportunity for a student to develop and use those skills necessary to lead a group or project. By providing leadership skills and opportunities for adolescents, it is believed that risk behaviors specific to substance use and violence will be reduced.

Data Collection

If this student leadership program is being implemented as a substance abuse prevention program, then all data related to substance use rates, amounts, and age of first use need to be collected. This often requires implementation of a regular schedule of student use surveys (see Resource R) every 2 or 3 years to monitor changes in use patterns. If this program is being implemented as a violence prevention program, then all data specific to harassment, fighting, or other identified violent acts need to be collected.

It will also be important to identify substance use rates, patterns, and age of onset within the subgroup of students participating in the student leadership program.

Goal of Student Leadership Program

The goal of this student leadership program is to provide, through leadership experiences, the skills necessary to resist and reduce substance use and/or violence.

Objectives

Process Objectives

1. By (specify date), two stipend positions will be created for staff to supervise a student leadership program.

2. By (specify date), 10 students will be participating in the student leadership program.

Outcome Objectives

1. Age of first use of alcohol among students involved with student leadership programs will increase by 0.5 year by (specify date).

2. Rate of tobacco use (violent behavior) by students involved with student leadership programs will decrease by 40% by (specify date).

Experimental Design

Our evaluation will use a control group with pre-, immediate post-, and delayed postmeasures. The control group will be composed of students from this district who are matched with our experimental group by age, gender, academic program, and extracurricular involvement.

Data on violent behaviors, substance use patterns, and age of first use will be collected via a self-report instrument from both the experimental and control groups prior to program initiation and will be similar to district-wide data already collected. These data will be re-collected immediately following student involvement in the program and at 6-month intervals thereafter.

Data from the experimental and control groups will be compared for similarities, differences, and significant differences. Data from these two groups and the general student population will also be compared for similarities, differences, significant differences, and any confounding variables.

Confounding variables to be examined will include the implementation of other leadership opportunities and any school-specific traumas or media events that might account for any across-the-board changes in student behavior.

▶ Second Thoughts

▶ Your *experimental design* needs to include the following five elements: (a) a program definition, (b) a data collection plan, (c) program goals, (d) program objectives, and (e) a description of the experimental design.

▶ The *program definition* needs to include the expected changes in student behavior that will result from program participation.

▶ The *data collection plan* needs to identify which data sets will most likely show change as a result of student participation. Where will you find these data? Who will collect them?

▶ When writing *program goals,* keep them to one sentence, making them broad, umbrella statements of the direction in which you would like to see student behavior move.

▶ Remember the *rule of fours,* and make your objectives measurable.

▶ The *description of your experimental design* should include your data collection schedule and what you will use as comparison data.

Crunching Your Numbers and Organizing Your Data

Aristotle maintained that women have fewer teeth than men; although he was twice married, it never occurred to him to verify this statement by examining his wives' mouths.

—Bertrand Russell

Compiling your data and making sense of them can be an overwhelming task, but well-summarized results of your program's outcomes will be enormously useful to you. Making sense of your data will lead to better programs. Simplifying your data for presentation will go far toward generating school and community support, advocating for additional funds, and making changes in your programs to meet the needs of participants. To summarize and report your program results effectively and accurately, all you need to know is how to count and do simple mathematics. Organizing your data is simply a process of grouping numbers, graphing trends, and otherwise making your program's results easier to look at and understand (see Figure 10.1).

To facilitate the process of data organization, start with a database/spreadsheet (computer) program that will allow you to sort data quickly by age, gender, grade level, ethnicity, or whatever other subgroup you are measuring. These programs are easy to use; you can learn to use them with competence in just a day. Enlist the help of your district computer classes or a community college if you need it.

Raw Data

The first major task is the organization and summarization of raw data to make it more understandable. Raw data can include all your demographic

■ **FIGURE 10.1.** Program Development: Flowchart 6

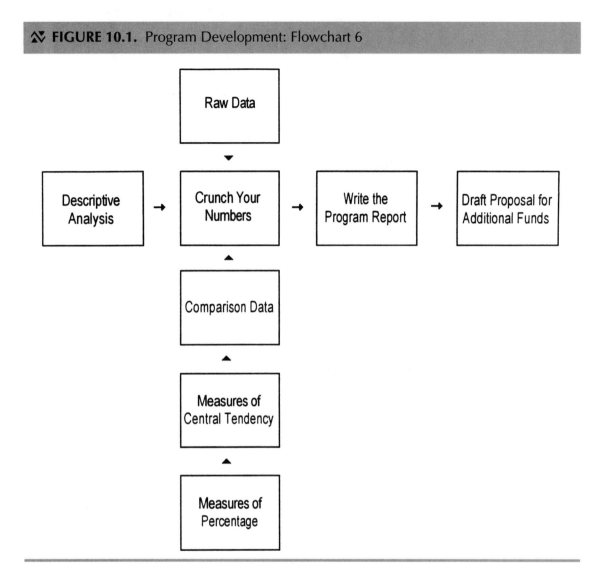

information, as well as the actual scores, grades, rates, and survey results for each person measured. Pages and lists of hundreds of raw scores are not only overwhelming, but they communicate nothing in that form. Raw data without some measure of central tendency, connection to a particular population, or comparison data are meaningless.

After you plug all the raw data into your database or spreadsheet program, organize them by grade, gender, and ethnicity. You'll want to be able to show that your population samples were random and representative of the overall population. See a sample demographic distribution in Table 10.1.

Now play around with the nondemographic numbers a bit. You'll want to organize these data in a few different ways to see what looks best or what most clearly shows progress with programming and trends in behaviors. Use the Sort function in your computer program and look for changes and patterns in different data groupings. For example: Did the boys do better than the girls? Did the older students change more than the younger students? Are the changes greater by age or by gender? What about comparing students

TABLE 10.1 Demographic Distribution of Students in Grades 6-12, Smallville School District, 2000-2001

Grade	Male	Female	Wh	AA	AI	PI	Hsp	Other	Total
6	108 (49%)	112 (51%)	212	2	1	3	1	1	220
7	96 (45%)	116 (55%)	208	3		1			212
8	90 (48%)	97 (52%)	183	1	1	1	1		187
9	93 (45%)	114 (55%)	204				3		207
10	99 (47%)	111 (53%)	207	1			1	1	210
11	102 (43%)	135 (57%)	235			2			237
12	114 (48%)	126 (52%)	237	2			1		240
Totals	702 (46%)	811 (54%)	1486 (98%)	9	2	7	7	2	1513

KEY:
Wh = Caucasian
AA = African American
AI = American Indian
PI = Pacific Islander (Cambodian, Hmong, Japanese, Korean, Laotian, Vietnamese)
Hsp = Hispanic (Cuban, Mexican, Puerto Rican, other Latin American)

who were in your program with students who weren't? How do your data look next to baseline data or other local school or community data? How about comparing your data with state or national data? You'll want to sketch some of this out on newsprint or graph paper to get a more accurate look.

Take your time with the review of all your raw data. Invite other people to look through them with you. Some schools and agencies even hire outside consultants to review the raw data and thus ensure they are getting an unbiased "read" of the numbers.

Descriptive Analysis ◀

A **descriptive analysis** is just what it says, a description, or word picture, of the overall program, goals, variables, and results. A descriptive analysis is a good way to begin a presentation of your data and includes the following general information:

▶ How many people were in the program? What ages?

▶ How long did the program last?

▶ How consistent were the results within the district/community or when compared with state or national numbers?

▶ Were any glitches found in the program, materials, or student experience?

▶ What are some raw numbers and percentages?

> **EXAMPLE**: This past fall, we ran groups for high school students who wanted to learn more about substance abuse because they had friends who were harmfully involved. We ended up with 30 interested students. We ran three "concerned persons" groups with 10 students in each. The groups met once a week for 10 weeks. We used our own school counselors as facilitators and had seven classroom aides trained in a group facilitation workshop so that they could cofacilitate. We ran into some problems with meeting space during the first 3 weeks but eventually found that we could use the small cafeteria early in the day without interruptions. Ninety-seven percent of students who began these groups finished. We collected student comments about their involvement in these groups to understand what they thought and felt about this program. All group participants were pretested on their own use behaviors, attitudes, and three other risk factors. We did short-term posttests 3 months after the groups had ended; they indicated that students who had completed these groups showed lower rates of drug use and other risk behaviors when compared with students who had not attended these groups. We will do another delayed posttest next fall at the 12-month mark. Let's take a closer look at some of our numbers . . .

A descriptive analysis begins your presentation of program results by providing an overview of where you've been and what you've done. This technique will focus your audience and help the numbers that follow make more sense to them. You may even want to submit it to newsletters or local newspapers that carry information on local events.

▣ Measures of Percentage

A *percentage* tells us what portion of the population is involved with the behavior we are measuring. Never underestimate the power of this simple piece of math. Most national and state data are summarized into percentages. Most people are used to seeing data in percentages. This is an easy calculation to do.

The first number you need is the number of students or individuals in the population you are serving, or your *target population*. In a school, this would be the total number of students. In a community, this would be the total number of individuals of a certain age or demographic. Depending on the program you are using, you might need to know the number of students at each grade level or at each age. These data are easy to find.

The second number you need is the number of students or individuals within your target population who are actually involved in the behavior you are measuring.

EXAMPLE 1: You have 124 ninth graders, 29 of whom indicate on a student survey that they are involved with using tobacco products. Divide 29 by the total number of students at that grade level surveyed, and multiply by 100. The result gives you the percentage of ninth graders who use tobacco products: (29 ÷ 124) x 100 = 23, or 23% of students are involved with using tobacco products.

EXAMPLE 2: A survey of 237 seventh and eighth graders shows that 12 of them have been involved in shoplifting and vandalism behaviors. What percentage of seventh and eighth graders are involved? Divide 12 by the total number of students, and multiply the result by 100. (12 ÷ 237) x 100 = 5, or 5% of seventh and eighth graders have been involved in shoplifting and vandalism behaviors.

Percentages are a good starting point. They can be used to summarize huge collections of raw data, thus allowing you to make statements like the following:

▶ 50% of students were involved with leadership activities during the 2001-2002 school year.

▶ 97% of students who began the fall program finished.

▶ Of the 48 involved students, 36 of them, or 75%, showed academic improvement.

▶ 81% of our students are not involved with marijuana use.

▶ 96% of community members between the ages of 12 and 18 have never been involved with petty crime.

▶ Attendance at the evening seminar represented 6% of district parents.

Statements of percentage can be powerful. They also need to be followed with a closer analysis of the data, including a measure of central tendency and comparison with other data.

Contingency Tables

Contingency tables provide a clear way to display your percentages. A **contingency table** presents the numbers and percentages of participants in

TABLE 10.2 Student Abstinence Rates With Three Intervention Programs, 1999-2000

	Students in ISS Intervention	Students in Support Groups	Students Receiving Individual Counseling	Totals
Students still abstinent at 6 months	20(17%)	29(48%)	20(67%)	69(33%)
Students not abstinent at 6 months (any use)	100(83%)	31(52%)	10(33%)	141(67%)
Totals	120(100%)	60(100%)	30(100%)	210(100%)

two or more groups. They are useful when categories are clear-cut, such as gender, age, and race. See Table 10.2 for an example of a contingency table displaying percentages.

From Table 10.2, it can be said that of the 60 students who participated in support groups, 31 of them, or 52%, were not abstinent 6 months later. It can also be said that of those students receiving individual counseling, 67% of them were abstinent 6 months later. This table shows that for this school, the in-school suspension (ISS) intervention was the least effective method of promoting long-term abstinence with the students.

◪ Measures of Central Tendency

A **measure of central tendency** is any measure that determines the average rate in a specified population. These include the mean, median, and mode. Measures of central tendency are used to summarize and describe huge data collections. Mean, median, and mode will each have direct application to your data. It is a good idea to figure out each of these three measures of central tendency because each will yield a slightly different kind of information.

Mean

The *mean* is the arithmetic average, the sum of all the scores divided by the total number of scores.

Sum of Scores ÷ Number of Scores = Mean

EXAMPLE: You have asked all 900 students in Grades 4 through 12 at what age they *first* used a tobacco product. If 60% of the 900 students have used tobacco products and answer this question, you will have 540 "ages." Add them all together, all 540 of them. If your final number is 5541, then divide that by the number of students (540) to get the average age (or "mean" age) at which tobacco-using students in your district first begin using tobacco products.

$$5541 \div 540 = 10.26$$

You can now say that the mean age at which students in your district begin to use tobacco products is just over 10 years old, or during fifth grade.

Determining the mean age at which certain behaviors begin is crucial in program planning. In this example, discovering that tobacco use begins in fifth grade tells this school that its tobacco prevention efforts must begin before the fifth grade to be effective.

One point of caution when determining mean ages: The mean can be influenced by extreme scores—in this case, ages of 17- and 18-year-olds. It is necessary to look at all the 540 "ages" to see how they are distributed across grade levels. This is best done with the use of a bar graph. By looking at the actual distribution of ages by grade level, you might find a different distribution that would have to be addressed by a different type of programming. Depending on your distribution, using the mode or median rather than the mean as a measure of central tendency might be better.

Median

The *median* is the single score that falls in the middle of all the data. To determine the median score, first type all your data into a database or spreadsheet program. Sort the data into numerical order, and select the central score. If you have 150 scores, the median is the 75th score. If you have 2400 scores, the median is the 1200th score. The median is almost always very close to the mean, or average score, for your group. It is particularly useful when dealing with ages. In the example for mean above, we ended up with an age of 10.26. That is an awkward number to use as an age. By determining the median, we would get a whole number that would be more meaningful.

Mode

The *mode* is the score or value most often given in a sample. This is not an average and is not calculated mathematically; it is simply the score that appears the greatest number of times.

EXAMPLE: You have asked all 900 students in Grades 5 through 12 at what age they *first* used marijuana. If 25% of students have used marijuana and answer this question, then you will have 225 "ages," or "age scores." List them all, sorted into groups by age. You can create a visual distribution by making a bar graph. The group that has the most in it will be the mode age at which students first start using marijuana in your district.

Determining the mode also has implications for program planning, as it will show you where clusters of certain behaviors are taking place. The mean age at which students start using marijuana might be 15, or tenth grade. In terms of programming, this would mean doing marijuana prevention in eighth or ninth grade. But by sorting your raw data and looking for the mode, you might find a smaller but significant cluster of marijuana users who are age 13, or in the eighth grade. This finding significantly affects program decisions because it means marijuana prevention that begins in ninth grade will miss a large group of early users. The mode suggests that marijuana prevention might be most effective, in this case, at the seventh-grade level.

◨ Comparison Data

Now is when you need all the comparison data you collected at the beginning of your data collection process. Percentages and measures of central tendency are meaningless without comparison data. What do you really know when you read that alcohol use rates for your high school students are at 33%, tobacco use rates are at 42%, and marijuana use rates are at 17%? Is this good or bad? Are your students using more or less than students in other communities or other states? Is this an increase or decrease in use since the last time you measured?

Developing programs aimed at reducing substance use and violent behaviors and precursor behaviors requires that you have all the baseline, local, state, and national data you can find. You hope your own data collection instruments were designed to collect similar data so that you will have accurate comparisons. For example, some state data reports on student violence or drug or alcohol use "within the past 30 days," "within the past year," and "lifetime." You will often find significant differences in these rates. Lifetime behaviors will be the highest measure; behaviors in the past 30 days is generally the lowest measure. To be able to compare your data with theirs, you need to have collected the same thing.

Figure 10.2 shows a graph of district and county rates of tobacco use. This shows the value of comparison data.

By adding comparison data, your local data now have more meaning. It can be said that Jamesville School has lower tobacco use rates than other schools in the county. A good next step would be to compare Jamesville data

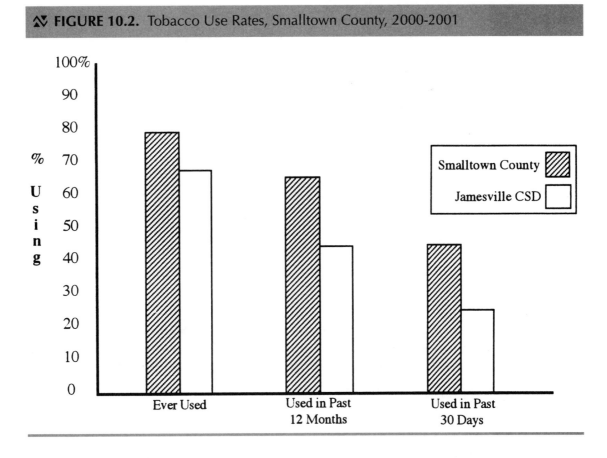

FIGURE 10.2. Tobacco Use Rates, Smalltown County, 2000–2001

with original baseline, statewide, and national numbers to see whether they have lower tobacco use rates than everyone else. Then Jamesville needs to start examining its programming, policies, and community efforts to determine *why* its use rates are lower so that it can continue being effective or improve on the effectiveness.

Charting and Graphing

As you can see from Figure 10.2, charts and graphs are easy for an audience to read and understand quickly. They allow for a lot of data to be shared through a single picture. They are necessary if you are trying to show trends or changes over time. A graph of student drug use over the past 5 years that shows steadily downward-sloping lines will speak volumes to the effectiveness of your program.

Frequency Distributions

Frequency distributions are charts or graphs prepared by grouping data into convenient intervals or frequencies. This task is especially easy to do if your data collection instrument was already broken into intervals. There are several ways to collect data in this way. Using a Likert-type scale (strongly

⚘ FIGURE 10.3. Question From a Student Use Survey

The Question:

Which category best describes your drinking behavior during the last 12 months?

☐ Never used

☐ Used infrequently (1-2 times)

☐ Used occasionally (2-3 times a month)

☐ Used regularly (2-3 times a week)

☐ Used often (nearly every day)

agree—strongly disagree) will do this. Having students rank themselves on a scale from 1 to 5, or having them select a category that best describes the frequency of their behavior, will also result in data that can be easily separated into frequency categories.

Let's examine a question from a student use survey and see how we can use the results to create a frequency distribution graph (see Figure 10.3).

A random sample of 221 students selected one of five different categories that best described their drinking behavior. Table 10.3 presents a summary of student responses to that question.

By grouping the scores of the 221 student responses, we can begin to see a pattern. This chart is not the best way to display this information. It can be

TABLE 10.3 Rates of Student Alcohol Use, 1999-2000

Category	Raw Scores	Percentage
Never use	70	32
Use infrequently (1-2 times in my life)	95	43
Use occasionally (2-3 times a month)	35	16
Use regularly (2-3 times a week)	16	7
Use often (nearly every day)	5	2
Totals	N = 221 students	100

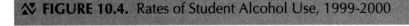

FIGURE 10.4. Rates of Student Alcohol Use, 1999-2000

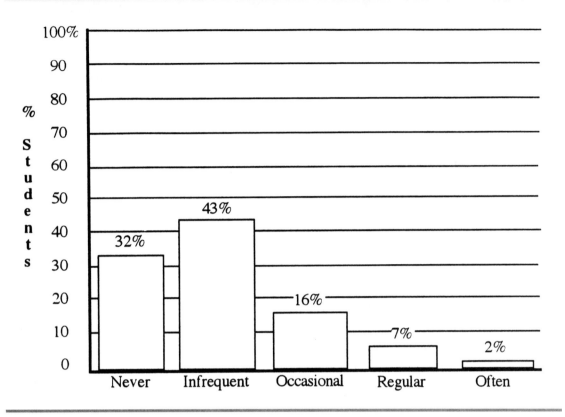

more clearly represented graphically, in the form of a distribution curve (see Figure 10.4).

By looking at this simple graph, we can clearly see that the majority of students, 75% of them, are either non-users or infrequent users of alcohol. Regular and heavy use accounts for less than 10% of the student population. Figure 10.4 allows us to feel good that so many students are not involved with high-risk drinking choices, but it also reminds us that we need an intervention and referral system in place for the 9% who are.

Presenting Community Change Data

It is difficult to measure community change as a result of programming. Chapter 8 discusses some quasi-experimental designs for measuring community change either by using **non-equivalent comparison groups** or by doing a **time series analysis.** Let's assume your community believes that by removing tobacco billboards, they will be able to reduce the sale of tobacco products. How will the effectiveness of that program be measured, and how will the data be presented?

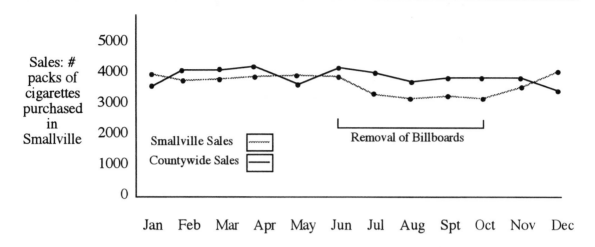

Â FIGURE 10.5. Sales of Packs of Cigarettes, Smallville, New York, 1999

Time Series Analyses

To start, data need to be collected for months (or years) prior to implementing the community intervention. In this case, we collected data on the total sales of cigarettes for each month during the year 1999. Those results are plotted in the graph in Figure 10.5. To show that our billboard removal intervention caused a decrease in cigarette sales, we need to show a dip, or reduction, in cigarettes during the time that the billboards are gone.

Non-Equivalent Comparison Groups

A similar or equivalent community can be used as a comparison group. If we select carefully, then most demographic details between the two communities will be similar, the only difference being the removal of tobacco billboards. A graph of those results, comparing the two communities, is shown in Figure 10.5.

From the results shown in Figure 10.5, we can conclude that a decrease in the sales of tobacco products took place during the period of billboard removal. We also can say that this decrease in sales looks as if it may have been specific to Smallville, where the billboards were removed. Can we say that removing the billboards *caused* the decrease in sales? No. We cannot attribute causation to this observation. Many other variables need to be explored as possible causes for this decrease in sales. For example, does the population of Smallville drop off during the summer when college students leave town? Does the neighboring community begin selling tobacco products at a different price during the summer? Time series analysis is a necessary tool when trying to show that a program had an impact in a larger population in response to a community-wide initiative, but remember that it simply shows patterns and trends, not causation.

Writing Your Program Report ◄

Every year, you will want to prepare a written report of your program's effectiveness. This report will contain a review of what you did, how it was received, the outcome measures of participant behavior, and recommendations for next year. This report will be kept on file either in the district office or in the school library where any interested person may have access to it and review your results. Assembling this annual report will prepare you for your public presentation of results, as well as give you a significant head start in completing competitive applications for additional funding. Your report needs to include the following items.

Title/Heading. This should go without saying, but it's a good reminder. Include a title page that states (a) the name of your program, (b) the dates covered by the report data, (c) the name(s) of the person(s) who conducted the program, (d) the name(s) of the person(s) who conducted the program assessment (indicate which one is the contact person), (e) the school or community where the program took place, and (f) the name of the funder or source of funds.

Descriptive Analysis. The first page should be a descriptive analysis of your program, similar to an abstract in a research report. This will probably take no more than one page. (Another example of a descriptive analysis for a substance abuse prevention program was presented earlier in this chapter.)

EXAMPLE: During the 2000-01 school year, we implemented bullying and teasing prevention programs in the elementary school grades. We implemented this program in eight classrooms, Grades 4 and 5. We trained eight of our classroom teachers as program facilitators and trained an additional eight classroom aides in this program so that they could co-facilitate the lessons. Fifteen 40-minute lessons were implemented once a week for 15 weeks. We ran into some problems with delayed arrival of materials but were able to borrow workbooks from a neighboring school until ours arrived. Ninety-nine percent of students who began these lessons finished them. We collected student comments about what they thought and felt about this program. All students were pretested on their own behaviors, attitudes, and experiences with conflict resolution, interpersonal communication, and three other risk factors. We collected data on the rates of teasing and bullying in the sixth through eighth grades. We did short-term posttests 3 months after lessons had ended to determine retention of skills and attitude change in the fourth and fifth graders. We will do another delayed posttest next fall at the 12-month mark. It will be most interesting to see whether our rates of bullying and teasing in the sixth through eighth grades drop during the next 3 years as students who have been through this program enter those grades. Implementation costs this year were high because we trained 17 people, but next year our only expenses will be replacement workbooks, cutting program costs by 75%.

Rationale. Describe the process of data collection and review and the conclusions that were drawn. List the original needs, goals, and objectives. Explain how and why this particular program was selected from among others. What specific features made this program best suited to your identified needs?

Program Assessment. Expand on what was said in your descriptive analysis. Specify what was collected as baseline data, any instruments developed or purchased, and a 3- to 5-year timeline for data collection. Describe any confounding variables you are trying to control through program design. Explain whether you have a control or comparison group, how it was selected, and how it will be used.

Results. Did you do what you planned to do? Are you accomplishing your goals? At what cost? If you have some outcome results, describe them. Remember to summarize raw data into percentages and to compare them with baseline or other local, statewide, or national data. Include graphs and charts and other visual materials you may have developed for presentations.

Remember to include a review of your time and cost effectiveness and improvements or changes that will be made in your program design as a result of this information. People, especially funders, like to see that you are being careful with how your money is spent.

Conclusions/Recommendations. A *conclusion* is a speculation about what your results mean. If your experimental design was good, you may even be able to attribute the trends in your data directly back to your programming. In most cases, it will be difficult to prove, definitely and without a doubt, that Program A *caused* Behavior Change B. The best that can be done is to observe, measure, and report on what *probably* happened to cause your results.

Include a section to speculate on what confounding variables may have affected your results. What changes or improvements will be tried next year? How will your data collection or program assessment plan be changed? Will programming be expanded into other grades or other areas of prevention? Identify two or three things that will be different next year based on the results of this year's program assessment.

Public Release of Results. Once the data have been tabulated and the committee members have drawn their conclusions about program effectiveness, experimental design, and directions for next year, it's time to make your results public. Before you do this, check to see who needs to approve the release of information from this final report. Who needs to be involved? Who sees it first? Does a higher governing board need to review and approve your report? How much of your report can be released to the press? Your school, agency, or funder may have an established protocol for how this is done. Prepare a press release based on the final report for release before your public presentation. See additional information on the public release of your results in Chapter 11.

Seeking Competitive Funds ◀

While program organization, annual reports, target audiences, data trends, and budget needs are still fresh in your mind, quickly draft a proposal for additional funds. It will never be easier, and you will be grateful that you have something "official" put down on paper. If you do this immediately after preparing your annual report, it will take you less than 1 hour.

The money is out there if you know where to look. Start with Resource BB and explore some on-line sources of funding. In addition to these federal and state funding sources, ample money may be available to you locally, beyond your school board and county government. Approach local businesses through the Chamber of Commerce, and speak at all the fraternal organizations. You may be surprised to find these groups looking for a good cause and only too happy to write you a check.

Many private foundations and corporations grant large sums of money to worthwhile prevention efforts. Large volumes outlining protocols for requests are printed annually—and are very expensive. To look at these resources for corporate and foundation giving, contact a Director of Institutional Grants at a local college or an administrator at the nearest intermediate educational agency for access to these books.

No matter where you decide to seek additional funding, you will need to write a proposal to take with you. It need be only a few pages long and should include the following:

▶ A description of the problem (based on data) and the target audience

▶ A description of the program and why it best meets the needs of this specific population

▶ Your program goal and a few measurable objectives

▶ A budget outline with your specific financial needs clearly stated (Specify whether you want them to foot the entire bill or whether you would like $2000 to cover just the training component or materials.)

> ► An outline of your evaluation plan and how you will measure success

> ► A letter or two of support from key organizations or individuals in your community

This proposal should be typed, clean, and very easy to read by skimming. Sometimes you only have a minute to make your pitch. When you make a specific, reasonable, and well-planned request for funds, you will be pleased with how generous your local resources can be. Always have a copy of your proposal in your briefcase; you never know who you'll end up sitting next to on the train!

▣ Second Thoughts

► Become familiar with basic database and spreadsheet programs.

► Summarize data in accurate and understandable ways by using percentages and measures of central tendency.

► Take the time to figure the mean, median, and mode for certain key behaviors.

► Remember that percentages alone do not show correlations.

► Always use relevant comparison data.

► Use charts and graphs to display often complex patterns and trends in an easy-to-understand way.

► When you are selecting or designing your data collection instruments, think ahead to how you will be using or synthesizing your resulting data. Select instruments that group or organize your data in the most logical ways.

► Create a written report and press release prior to giving your annual public presentation.

► Write a proposal for additional funding *right now*, while all the data, target audiences, trends, and budget needs are still fresh in your mind.

► Explore all protocols for release of annual report data, and adhere to them.

► Back up all your data!

Public Presentation of Your Results

Nothing is more dangerous to a new truth than an old error.

—Goethe, *Proverbs in Prose*

Your results, presented well, will go a long way toward establishing support for your program(s). A solid presentation will make a compelling argument to local officials, parents, teachers, community agencies, school administration, and funders to continue supporting prevention. The ultimate goals of your presentation are (a) to make your materials relevant to your audience, (b) to be accurate, and (c) to keep it interesting. A lot of work goes into publicly reporting the results of your program (see Figure 11.1). The following guidelines will ensure maximum success (*Making the Most of Your Presentation*, 2000).

Guidelines for Ensuring Presentation Success

Know Your Ultimate Goal

Ask yourself why you are making this presentation in the first place. Are you trying to sell the program? Inform the audience? Justify your job? Persuade listeners for additional funding or for a change in program direction? Motivate the audience to take action? First, describe exactly what result you want. All presentation content should support the results you have in mind.

⚡ FIGURE 11.1. Program Development: Flowchart 7

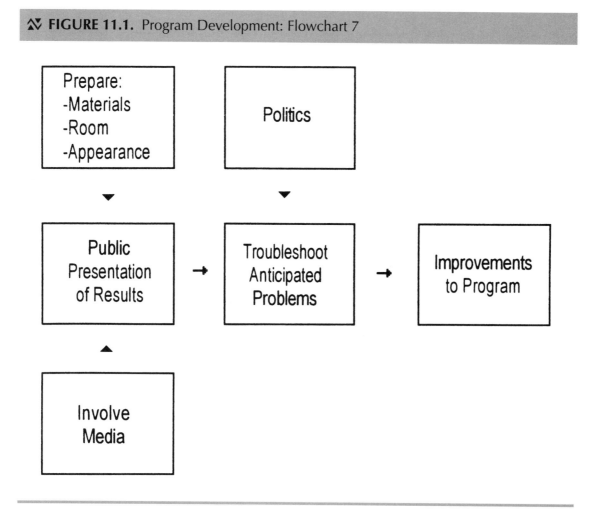

Outline Your Presentation

Never step in front of an audience unprepared. At a minimum, your presentation outline should include the items listed in Table 11.1.

Emphasize that the impact of prevention programming is community-wide, not just school based. Conclude by identifying strengths that were uncovered, logical next steps, and areas for growth.

Know Your Audience

To whom are you speaking? A presentation to elected officials will be quite different from a presentation to youth. How large will the audience be? What is their connection to the materials you are presenting? Will this program cost them money? Will they be able to participate? Do they have any prior experience with this subject matter? Do you need to address any potential misinformation or rumor? Do they have any underlying concerns, like

TABLE 11.1 Minimum Contents for Your Presentation Outline

Content	Example
a. Tell who you are and why you are qualified to give this presentation. What are your connections to different groups within the school community?	You are not just the program director. You may also be a parent, grandparent, community member, or business owner.
b. Identify the topic and why it is of interest/importance to this particular audience.	"I'm here to talk about _____ and how it affects _____."
c. Describe the extent of the problem with data from two or more sources for support. Identify the population to be served on the basis of the data.	Use baseline data compared with similar local, state, or national data. Highlight when the first signs of this behavior begin.
d. Describe the effects of the problem that would be most relevant to your audience.	If you're talking to teachers, then this has a direct impact on academic achievement and behavior in the classroom. If you are talking to a fraternal organization, then approach this problem from the perspective of community impact, vandalism, safety, or impact on local business. Funders like to see that prevention is significantly less expensive than treatment.
e. Introduce solutions to this problem. Be specific. Name programs, and provide a descriptive analysis of what has happened so far.	Describe your program here. Introduce program goals and objectives.
f. Briefly describe your experimental design. Although this is quite important, most audiences are not interested beyond knowing that it is being done.	Use one transparency to show what data you are collecting and how you hope these will show program effectiveness.
g. Present results. Share program success.	If you have postprogram data, display them with comparison data to show that student risk behaviors are decreasing.

fears of increasing taxes, poor previous experiences with prevention programs and personnel, or general distrust of "outsiders"? Will your presentation be seen as controversial? The more you know about the audience, the more prepared you can be.

Know Your Physical Setting

Know where you will be speaking, and visit the location before your presentation if you can. Will you be in a classroom, auditorium, cafeteria, or gym? How large is the room? Will you need a microphone? (When in doubt, use one!) Will the audience be arranged at tables, desks, or just in rows of chairs? Can the furniture be moved, and do you need to move it ahead of time? Is there an echo, a ventilation fan, a PA system, or other auditory distraction? What audiovisual equipment is available, and how will you arrange to have it there on the day of your presentation? Don't assume that the overhead projector you see there today will be there next week for your presentation—ask. Will everyone be able to hear you, see you, and see your materials?

The day of your presentation, get there early to make sure the room is properly set up and everything works. Actually turn on the equipment and go to the back of the room to check for readability. Make sure that water is available for the speaker and that you know where the exits and bathrooms are.

Check Your Timing

How much time you are given determines what you will be able to do and what content you will be able to share. Do you have a deadline? Are you following another speaker, and how long did that person talk? Does your audience need a break before you begin? What length of presentation is the audience used to or expecting? If there is a set time frame for your presentation, does that include time for questions and answers? If not, you need to build that in. Make sure a clock or watch is visible to you so that whatever your time limits may be, you don't ever go over.

Be Focused and Concise

It's been said that the average adult has an attention span of only 12 minutes. That means you need to have six to eight points to make and not spend more than 10 minutes on any one point. Keep it short and simple while still covering important information. It helps if you diversify your presentation style, including short anecdotes and video clips. Involve the audience as well, giving them a short quiz or calling on them to share relevant examples. Increased audience participation will lead to increased attentiveness and retention of the material.

Prepare Handouts, Overheads, and PowerPoint (PPT)

Handouts, overheads, and PPT all serve to improve a presentation by expanding the avenues through which you share information. A portion of your audience will learn best by listening to you speak. Others will need to see the information written down on the overheads or in a handout. Because these materials are a direct reflection of you as the presenter, and your expertise and credibility, take the extra time to make them great.

Transparencies/PPT

▶ Use an 18-point font or larger.

▶ Only put three to five items on any one sheet/screen.

▶ Use bulleted items; they are easy for the eye to read.

▶ Use high-contrast colors with the writing in the darker color. Stay away from yellows, oranges, and reds.

▶ Prepare all transparencies ahead of time; handwritten overheads are unacceptable.

▶ Make sure transparencies are error free.

Handouts

▶ Make handouts ahead of time.

▶ They must be neatly typed and error free.

▶ Never hand out copies that are grainy, smudged, handwritten, or otherwise difficult to read. Take the time to retype and make clean copies.

▶ Use bulleted items; they're easy for the eye to read.

▶ Remember that few people want to read the whole report; they trust you to summarize the important points in your handouts.

▶ Include photographs of the program in progress if you have some.

▶ Make sure you have enough for everyone.

Know Your Material and Keep It Accurate

A knowledgeable presenter can be very persuasive. The person making this presentation should also be trustworthy and competent, as he or she will reflect on your program and the entire evaluation. Don't agree to make this presentation unless you're confident you can support everything you say with research and can answer (or refer) any questions that may be asked. Prepare to defend the accuracy and validity of your instruments (especially student surveys) and other data collection processes. Know when a question is beyond the scope of your presentation or your area of expertise, and refer the asker to a source for accurate answers.

Keep your materials and any conclusions you might draw as accurate as possible. Anything you say that is unbelievable to your audience will hurt your credibility and lower their trust for what preceded and what will follow. If the data you are presenting really are difficult to believe, make sure you use supporting data for validation.

Involve Youth

It is difficult and sometimes unfair to describe your entire program with a series of charts and graphs. The "feel" of your program and its impact on the lives of the youth who are involved could be lost. If you have the time, consider involving program participants in the development and presentation of program data. Participants may choose to highlight different program aspects and may have short anecdotes to share. Youth involvement will add energy to your presentation.

Present Often

Be prepared to make frequent presentations on your program's progress. Prepare monthly or quarterly summaries for the district newsletter or student newspaper. Provide short updates at occasional faculty meetings. Attend PTA meetings, and present your data there when appropriate. Not only will this increase program visibility and buy-in and reduce resistance to future prevention efforts, but these constant reports and mini-presentations will keep you extremely familiar with your program data and will keep you in shape for the "big" presentations. Knowing what sorts of questions you can anticipate from different audiences and describing your data in different ways will improve the confidence and accuracy of your presentations.

Look the Part

How you look and how you sound are, unfortunately, more memorable than what you actually say. During the first 90 seconds that an audience sees you, they will make certain decisions about you. First impressions are very powerful and difficult to overcome. If their first impression is that you are sloppy and disorganized, they may not take very seriously what you have to say. You want to control for all the visual and vocal variables so that the content of what you're saying is what gets remembered.

Physical Appearance. Always dress a step above how you anticipate your audience will be dressed. Keep your hair out of your face. Control your physical image as much as possible so that no one notices it.

Women should wear stockings, keep their skirts on the longer side, avoid displaying too much cleavage, and wear jewelry that isn't too noisy or too large or distracting. Bare midriffs are out, as are blue jeans, shorts, and open-toed shoes. All these things will lower the credibility of the speaker.

Men should wear a shirt with a collar. Sneakers are out, as are blue jeans, shorts, baseball caps, sandals, going without socks, and going without a belt. Even if you don't wear it, at least have a jacket in the car, just in case.

Posture. Face your audience, with your feet planted parallel and apart. Don't shift your weight over to one foot or cross your feet while you're talking. Stay in one place, "home base," and as you move around always return to that spot. Try not to stand behind anything. Often a room will be arranged so that the speaker can stand behind a podium or a table. Don't do this. You will be much more effective with nothing between you and your audience.

Eye Contact. Remember to look at your audience. Don't look over their heads at the back of the room. Try not to look only at one or two people or, worse, stare down a single participant. That will make your audience uncomfortable, especially the person you are staring at! Make eye contact with each member of your audience for 3 to 5 seconds and then move on. Be aware if you are favoring one side of the room over another; this is common and something you do not want to do.

Body Movement. Use your arms and hands to enhance your presentation. Point to things with your hands, gesture, move them around as naturally as if you were in your backyard telling your neighbor a story. Most of us, when in front of an audience, suddenly have no idea what to do with these heavy appendages that are hanging at our sides. We become tremendously self-conscious about them and start doing weird things. We hold them stiffly at our sides, occasionally flapping them at the wrists like penguins. We shove them into our pockets where we are likely to fiddle with our keys. We cross them over our chests or, worse, our genitals, letting our audience know that we feel completely naked up there. Keep your hands out of your pockets, and try not to let them touch each other. Practice in front of a mirror to get some of your natural movement back.

Other body movements that can be effective are leaning in toward your audience, taking steps toward them, or even standing in the audience, always returning to home base.

Face and Hands. Facial expressions are always good; the more the better. They will entertain and bring life to your presentation. They always look less extreme to your audience than they feel to you. Hands are also very expressive. Try to keep them from touching you, though. Standing in front of an audience is not the time to pick your nose or ears, scratch anywhere, or rearrange underclothing. Remember where you are.

Volume. Make sure you speak loudly enough for everyone to hear; otherwise you will lose your audience. Don't shout. If necessary, use a microphone. If you've never used one before, practice ahead of time; microphones can be temperamental. Even more effective is varying your volume while you are speaking. For example, present the data in a normal tone of voice and then add, with a little less volume, "And you know what else we found . . . (dramatic pause)?" By lowering your volume, you have achieved what is called the "conspiratorial tone." Everyone in your audience is now anticipating that they will be let in on a juicy secret. Great! You've got their attention. Variation in volume will help maintain their interest.

Rate. Not too slow or too fast. Like volume, varying the rate of your speech can be a great technique for maintaining interest.

Pauses and Fillers. Fillers are the death of any presenter. Remember that teacher you had in high school who used to say "ah," "um," "you know," or "OK" just about every other word? Chances are you spent more than one class period counting the "OKs" rather than paying attention to what was being said. Fillers are distracting. Unfortunately, you seldom know when they are a part of your own speech, and even if they are not, they may appear when you speak publicly. Videotaping yourself is an effective tool for helping break this habit. Enlist a friend to be the audience as you practice your presentation; have him or her let you know every time you say something like "um," "OK," "ah," "you know," and so on.

Pauses, in contrast, can be very dramatic. If you lose your place in your notes, just take a second to collect yourself. What seems like an eternity to you, the speaker, is just a moment of silence to your audience. Use pauses after you ask rhetorical questions, after you present data (to let them sink in), or while waiting for an audience response.

Provide Access to Results

Results of your program outcome studies should be made available to all interested persons. Some will want to examine the full report rather than the summary handed out at your presentations. Have the full report available in the district office or library, and let the public know it is available to them. Make sure all necessary protocol was followed before making this report available to the general public.

Be Impartial

Impartial reporting means taking care to report just the facts as they really turned out. Avoid distorting, skewing, or misrepresenting your results because of personal feelings. This program may be your baby, but if it has had no measurable impact on reducing student drug use, then that is what you must report. Perhaps you dislike the program intensely, but if it is effective in reducing aggression in students, then that is what you are obligated to report.

Do not conceal negative results. Instead, present them and explain any planned program changes that will be made to compensate for or correct the problem. "These results show us that we may have focused this program at the wrong age group, so we will be making the following program adjustments."

Anticipate Politics

It's always true, everywhere and always, that a person or group of persons will not like you or agree with your work. Anticipate these persons or groups, and do your best to involve them in early and sustained dialogue throughout the process of developing your program and measuring its success. By listening to their concerns from the start, you will be able to anticipate their counterarguments and counteragendas. You may also discover that all parents and community members, no matter which end of the religious or political spectrum they are on, are arguing for the same things: the health and safety of their children. Sometimes it's just a matter of listening to each other and changing our language.

> **EXAMPLE:** A community had implemented an elementary grades, skills-based prevention program. Almost immediately a particular church group claimed that the materials were "satanic" and that the families were going to pull their children out of school unless the school removed the program. The church group was well organized and had provided the local media with information on how this church had removed this program from schools in different communities across the country. The school's health advisory committee met with this church group. They learned that the concerns of this church involved the use of relaxation exercises that used "guided imagery" techniques. The school agreed to teach a different relaxation skill and eliminated the guided imagery.

This community was able to listen to both sides and achieve a compromise that was beneficial to the students because they were still able to learn a stress management skill. The solution turned out to be simple. This situation could have been avoided if the church community had been involved from the beginning in data review and program selection.

It is also possible that genuinely unreasonable people in your school-community intend to sabotage your prevention efforts. Get to know them, their agendas, and their causes. The more you understand, the better able you will be to prevent their biased interpretation of community data, their misapplication of data or results, and even their possible attempts to interfere with program implementation and data collection.

⊳ Using the Media

The term *the media* includes all forms of mass communication in your community—school and community newsletters, posters and billboards, radio, local cable television, newspapers, and magazines. Media partnerships will be a benefit to you as you begin publicizing your program's activities and results. By effectively using media outlets in your school community, you will be able to communicate with many more people about your prevention efforts and generate more widespread support.

The key word here is *effectively*. Many of us have had the unpleasant experience of being misquoted or of having media cover the problems with youth rather than the successes. This can be turned around so that local media become your advocates (*Working With the Media*, 2000).

Know Where to Send Information

Knowing where to send information that you want printed, broadcast, or displayed is important. Your school or agency may already have established media contacts, so check those first. To expand your contacts, start by looking through the telephone book. Call the media outlet and ask for "public affairs" or the "marketing department" or "an editor." Find out the name of the person to submit news items to and the regular deadlines for going to press or on-air. Some local newspapers have a special pull-out section on school news or on youth activities once a week. Find out how to get your news included there.

Establish a Single Media Contact

Establish a single media contact between your program/school/agency and the media. Some schools have a public relations officer who does this. Find out who this person is, or designate someone. By having a single person acting as a liaison, you can reduce duplication and can better control the material that is released.

Keep an up-to-date media contact file, and make sure each name receives all mailings you send out related to your program. If you have a VIP list for events, workshops, or presentations, make sure to include your media contacts on that list.

Write Impressive Press Releases

Keep your message powerful and focused. Think headlines: "Peer Mediation Group Reduces Fighting," "Students Help Students Quit Smoking." Most news information on youth is positive. Let the media know about students' contributions, successes, energy, talents, and enthusiasm.

When writing a press release, use the "inverted pyramid" style, putting the most important facts first, (who, what, when, where, how, and why), followed by the less important and finally the least important information. That way, a reader just skimming through the newspaper will still get the most important facts. Limit your press release to no more than two typed pages (double-spaced, single-sided). Proofread for spelling and grammar. Submit your press release promptly; old news is no news.

Use a Variety of Media

In addition to local school and community newsletters, don't forget about local cable television stations. They can be very receptive to school and community news. Remember to consider Web sites as well. Most schools now have Web sites that contain a current events section. Don't underestimate the power of letters to the editor or supermarket bulletin boards. If that is where the community is used to seeing news and events, then that is where you have to put your stuff.

> **EXAMPLE:** One community had a difficult time getting attendance at their annual meetings to report program outcomes publicly. They had sent flyers home to all parents of students in Grades 7 through 12, put up posters around town, and even had spots on the local radio station, but still attendance was low. This is an all too familiar situation. During focus groups, they asked students and community members for ideas to improve attendance. Students said they got most of their news on current events from "the underpass," a tunnel that passed under the main road through town. The school was on the south edge of town, and nearly all students and many adults walked through the underpass twice a day. The committee visited the underpass and found not only that it was functioning as an informal bulletin board of community events but also that the walls had been painted with murals advertising the bigger events. They partnered with the school art department, purchased paint, and advertised their next annual meeting on the underpass. Attendance improved.

Record All Media Coverage You Receive

Keep track of all radio, television, and newspaper coverage. Keep scrapbooks with clippings. Keep track of the telephone calls and mail you get in response to television, radio, newspaper, or advertisements, including the name and address of the person responding. You can use this group in the future to survey what made the media spot most effective and what the responders learned from it. This information will help you work even more effectively with the media.

Be Persistent

Getting media coverage will sometimes require persistence. Remember to follow up on all telephone calls and to return every telephone call you get from a media outlet. Keep the local media on your mailing list informed of your program activities, even if they don't often show up to cover events. You never know when it's going to be a slow news day or they need to do a feel-good piece. Make sure that you and your programs are familiar names. Name recognition is important because the day will come when they need a story or your program fits the profile of a piece they are working on and they'll think of you.

To increase the media's interest in your program, let them know that this program deals with an important, timely, problem/solution of concern to the larger community, that it is effective, and that the story to tell is an interesting one. What makes your prevention efforts stand out as different from the dozens of others taking place in surrounding communities? Provide photographs of program activities if you have them.

Include the Media in Other Roles

Chances are good that you have a board of directors, an advisory council, or a committee that helps plan and promote programming. Include a local media person on this committee but in the role of a "parent" or a "community representative." Remember to recruit from local businesses—media included—when you need volunteers for program events.

The results of your program assessment, whether presented by you or reported by the media, will be the foothold you need to generate community support and increased funding. Take the extra time to prepare both written and spoken presentations of results so that the messages that are released into your community are accurate and highlight the effectiveness of your work.

⯈ Second Thoughts

▶ Present results of your program's effectiveness in an accurate and confident manner. This will win support for your program.

▶ Be familiar with your audience, the room, all the materials, and audiovisual equipment you will be using *before* you start presenting.

▶ Involve youth in your presentation of program results as a way of increasing energy and interest.

▶ Control for as many variables in your presentation style and appearance as you can to ensure that what is remembered is what you *said*, not how you looked.

▶ Establish media partnerships by using a variety of traditional and nontraditional media outlets.

▶ Anticipate politics: Forewarned is forearmed.

Troubleshooting Your Results 12

People in general have no notion of the sort and amount of evidence often needed to prove the simplest fact.
—Peter Moore Latham, *Collected Works*

How smoothly did the program development and measurement process go during the first year? Chances are good that even if you were able to complete your original plan and timeline, it was a rough and disorganized process. This chapter reviews a few common problems and offers solutions for simplifying or repairing your process.

Problems and Solutions for ◀ Simplifying or Repairing Your Process

Disorganized Data Collection

Accurate data collection is the most important part of conducting an accurate assessment of your program's effectiveness. It is also the most difficult part and the piece that is done with the least accuracy and follow-through. One simple way to improve this aspect of your program assessment is to standardize the data collection methods across all your prevention programs.

Standardize Data Collection

Most program directors keep records of basic program data—how many participants; their age, gender, race, and other demographics; referral sources; disposition of the case; and more. As you may have already discovered, this type of data collection is not standardized because it comes from different programs and different people and uses paperwork reflecting the needs of different funders. This mix results in disorganized data that are difficult to use and time-consuming to sort through. If a process is difficult and time-consuming, it is less likely to get done.

By standardizing a data collection system across all prevention programs, you will collect a great deal of valuable information. Standardizing your record keeping involves creating a form that meets the needs of all program facilitators and all funders. All persons doing prevention programming need to sit together with all their various data collection forms and develop a single form that reflects everyone's needs. Information that you will want may include the following:

Age	Grade	Residence	Length of involvement
Ethnicity	Gender	Academic status	Reason for involvement
Disposition	Program	Referral source	

This standardization can be further simplified by converting it to a user-friendly checkoff form so that information can be easily collected. Even simpler, have all participants in prevention activities and programs complete a form at the beginning of each prevention program. The checkoff format will also make the data easy to categorize and enter into a database program (see the sample in Resource CC).

This information alone will allow you to evaluate many aspects of your programming:

▶ Is programming reaching your target population? (The right age, gender, race, or specific academic status?)

▶ Are any groups being underserved (or overserved)? (Are your program participants 90% female? Only in ninth grade?)

▶ Have changes occurred in the population being served? (Are their grades going up or down? Are you getting them from a different referral source?)

▶ Are the referral sources the ones you expected, or do you need to do more advertising or outreach? (Does everyone know about your program and how to refer students into it? Should you be getting referrals from any specific places but are not?)

Create a Timeline for Data Collection

Before the program year begins, create a timeline for data collection (see Table 12.1). Identify what data are to be collected, by whom, and by when. During the first year, pay close attention to where you get crunched for time, and make adjustments for next year (see the "Data Collection Timeline Worksheet" in Resource DD).

TABLE 12.1 Data Collection Timeline

Date Due	Task	Responsible Person(s)
09-01	Administration of teacher pretest on classroom techniques	Prevention Specialist
09-01	Student support group participants pretest	Guidance Staff
10-01	Student support group participants en-route feedback	Guidance Staff
10-01	Administration of student use survey	Building Administrator
12-01	Student support group posttest	Guidance Staff
12-01	Police report data on juvenile crimes	Prevention Specialist
12-01	Probation office data on PINS	Prevention Specialist
12-01	Student focus groups to monitor concerns and attitude change	Prevention Specialist, Guidance Staff
05-02	Student focus groups to monitor concerns and attitude change	Prevention Specialist, Guidance Staff
06-02	Administration of teacher posttest on use of classroom techniques	Prevention Specialist
06-02	Police report data on juvenile crimes	Prevention Specialist
06-02	Probation office data on PINS	Prevention Specialist
06-02	Student support group delayed posttest	Guidance Staff
07-02	Public report of program activities and progress	Building Administrator
07-02	School discipline records—annual summary	Administrative Secretary
04-03	Administration of student risk and asset survey	Building Administrator
10-04	Administration of student use survey	Building Administrator
04-06	Administration of student risk and asset survey	Building Administrator
10-07	Administration of student use survey	Building Administrator

Youth Behavior Worsens

Your results may indicate that the behaviors and attitudes you targeted worsened after program implementation. For a few reasons, you need not be too concerned about this during the first year.

1. Once you isolate, define, and begin collecting data on specific behaviors, it is likely that all your numbers will increase during the first year. This does not always represent an increase in the actual behavior. It's likely that observation and reporting procedures have improved, accounting for the higher numbers. Seek out validation data. Chances are your data will level off during the next few years.

2. No matter what program you put in place, risk behaviors will continue to increase between the fourth and ninth grades. The increase will always be there at that age. The prevention program needs to show that it has either delayed the increase or reduced the rate of increase.

3. Your increase may still be less than state or national increases during that year or with that age-group. Use comparison data.

If the data still suggest that youth risk behaviors increased or did not change after program implementation, then you need to reexamine your program content and implementation before replacing it.

Program Appears Ineffective

If student behaviors have not changed or have worsened during the program period, it may look as if your program has been ineffective. Before jumping to this conclusion, examine the following program elements to see whether you can make changes for the next year.

Recheck Your Data Interpretation

Check all your data to make sure they are valid and reliable. It is possible that the program appears ineffective because data are being misinterpreted.

Review the Research

Has any research been done on this particular program? What does the research say about this program's effectiveness with the population you are serving? Is the research conclusive? If no research has been conducted on this program or technique, then you need to either conduct your own or shop for a new program.

Rethink Teacher Preparation

Have the teachers and other staff who implemented this program been properly trained? Training in the specific program is best. Set aside money to provide this type of training before program implementation next year.

Implement the Program as Recommended

Has this program been implemented as recommended? Has a specified timeline been followed, and have all materials been used properly? If it has been hit-and-miss or if presenters/facilitators have taken liberties and changed the content or materials, then you have not had faithful program implementation and will not get the expected results. Next year, use classroom observers and teacher implementation logs so that you can see where the difficulty in implementation is and how you can fix it.

A Shooting or Similar Tragedy

Isolated incidents like shootings will happen. They are tragic. First, make sure your district crisis plan is used to take care of the students and staff, control media reports, and provide services to families and other community members.

A tragedy that occurs does not mean that your program is ineffective or that prevention in your community failed. It simply means that one person who needed mental health services didn't get identified in time. Run student and teacher focus groups to determine what type of supplemental programming or training they would like to have to deal with this crisis, or what they think could be done to prevent future, similar tragedies. Respond promptly with support, training, policy changes, and press releases.

Occasional tragedies and crises occur in all communities. They do not mean that prevention programming is failing or is ineffective.

Hammered by the Media

Unfortunately, the media may intentionally spin data to capture headlines. Fringe groups may also use this tactic as a way of expanding public support for their agendas. Make sure you know the media contacts in your area and are in constant touch with them. Have them on all your mailing lists, and provide them with as much current and accurate information about your program as possible. Fax them press releases as often as you have an interesting story. If you have built this base of support, it will be more difficult for a fringe group to misrepresent your programs.

The sensationalizing of data seems to be a current trend. It is far more interesting to report that use of inhalant drugs has increased 30% among eighth graders than it is to say that 94% of students through Grade 12 have never even tried inhalants. Before you release sensational student information or stories, review the following points:

► Check all your data, especially those that differ significantly from the norm, to determine whether they truly represent student behavior.

▶ Refuse to exaggerate, highlight, or focus on the atypical or "sensational" student behaviors. They will be in a decided minority and will not represent the general youth population in your school or community.

▶ Choose to highlight behaviors that are safe or prosocial. These behaviors will more likely represent the norms of your student population.

▶ Rephrase data in a more proactive way. Instead of saying, "17% of our high school students are smoking marijuana," try saying, "83% of our high school students are NOT smoking marijuana."

The *Chicago Sun-Times* was radical in its decision not to give front page coverage to either the Colorado or Arkansas school shootings. The editors cited, among other reasons, a danger that publicity surrounding such attacks could be contributing to the phenomenon. Time has proved their decision and their reasons for it to be correct.

Data Used in a Misleading Way

Twisting data or using it out of context is the worst case scenario with the media or with fringe groups. Sometimes misleading data are used on purpose as a way of making program results look different from what they are. Sometimes it happens by accident because the person preparing the material isn't familiar with handling data or preparing charts and graphs. Either way, you never want your data presented in a way that does not show the truth. Data can be used in several misleading ways.

Skewed Data

If your original data sample was not random and did not represent the entire population being served, then the resulting data will also not represent the overall population. For example, if you have a population that is 50% males but your data sample is only 20% males, then your data do not represent a random or representative sample. That means you cannot draw any conclusions between your results and the general population of your school community.

EXAMPLE: A school district intending to do a thorough student use survey sent home active parent consent letters. It received about a 75% return on those letters. Personnel did no follow-up letters or telephone calls to get the remaining 25% returned because they assumed that 75% was a large enough sample. They administered the survey to the 75% of students who had returned their permission slips. The resulting data showed that the school district had the lowest violence and substance abuse rates and risk factors in the state. They were thrilled! Looking more closely at their data, though, they discovered that the demographic information from the survey

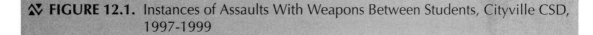

FIGURE 12.1. Instances of Assaults With Weapons Between Students, Cityville CSD, 1997-1999

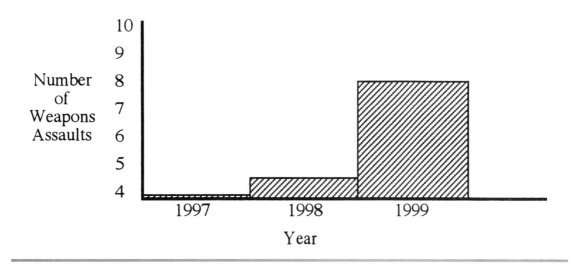

did not match their demographic information from other sources. It seems that the 25% of unreturned surveys were from homes that had some disorganization or chronic problem. Not only did these families need the follow-up to get the parent consent letter returned, but these were the students responsible for the greatest percentage of other risk behaviors as well. Without their participation in the survey, the results were invalid. As much as this district's administration would have liked to have concluded that their programs were effective in reducing violence and substance abuse, they could not. They could only conclude that in organized families who were able to return the permission slips on time, use rates and rates of violence were lower than state norms.

Misleading Charts and Graphs

Creating charts and graphs requires attention to detail. One common error is to provide a chart or graph of raw data with no comparison data (see Figure 12.1).

Figure 12.1 communicates that what looks like a significant increase in the frequency of weapons assaults has taken place. That is exactly what this chart was designed to do—to shock the audience. This sort of chart is often used to make a plea for expanded programming, increases in personnel, or increased funding. Although these may be accurate numbers, this is a dishonest way of presenting the data because it is intended to be deceptive.

One way to correct these data is to begin the vertical, or *y*, axis at 0 rather than at 4. This will normalize the distribution. When done this way, the data will appear less sensational and more accurate (see Figure 12.2).

These data could be further clarified by transforming them from raw data into percentages or per capita rates. By doing this, we can take into

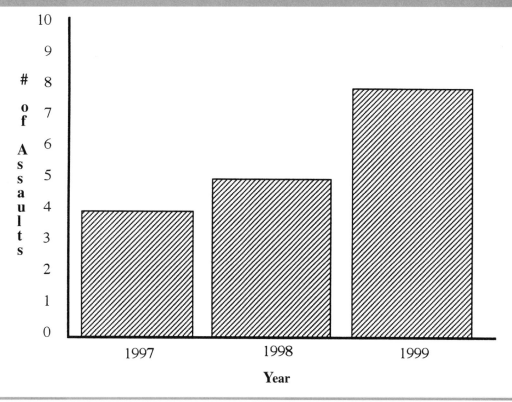

꙰ FIGURE 12.2. Instances of Assaults With Weapons Between Students, Cityville CSD, 1997-1999

account any increases in population that may explain increases in our raw data. Larger communities will have higher numbers of actual incidents of violence and substance abuse. The raw numbers will be higher than in a smaller community, but the percentages will be similar. The raw numbers will also change when a community grows or shrinks, but the percentages should remain fairly constant. For example, if our population grew by 10%, we could expect that our incidents of violence and substance abuse would also increase by 10%. If our rate of violence increased by 8% but our population grew by 12%, then we actually have a *decrease* in our per capita rate of violence. Start by creating a chart of information (see Table 12.2).

From the data in Table 12.2, it can be accurately stated that far less than 1% of the student population at Cityville High School has been involved in a weapons assault (0.032%, 0.036%, and 0.047%, respectively). If we had the same raw number of incidents at Farmville, a much smaller school, the data might be more remarkable (see Table 12.3).

From the data in Table 12.3, it can also be accurately stated that less than 1% of the student population at Farmville High School has been involved in a weapons assault (0.37%, 0.46%, and 0.73%, respectively). If we compare the per capita rates of weapons incidents between the two schools, however, we can see that Farmville is a far more dangerous place. We can't actually say that Farmville High School is "dangerous," because the chance of a student being involved in a weapons-related incident is less

TABLE 12.2 Cityville High School per Capita Rate of Weapons Incidents

Cityville High School	Total Enrollment	Percent Increase in Enrollment	Number of Weapons Incidents	Per Capita Rate of Weapons Incidents
1997	12,211		4	1 in 3052
1998	13,740	12.5	5	1 in 2748
1999	16,882	22.8	8	1 in 2110

TABLE 12.3 Farmville High School per Capita Rate of Weapons Incidents

Farmville High School	Total Enrollment	Percent Increase in Enrollment	Number of Weapons Incidents	Per Capita Rate of Weapons Incidents
1997	1057		4	1 in 264
1998	1082	2.3	5	1 in 216
1999	1093	1.0	8	1 in 137

than 1%, but it *is* more dangerous than the school in a neighboring community.

Adding comparison data will put these numbers into better perspective by showing them against a backdrop of baseline, local, state, or national trends. We can also use other forms of violent behavior for comparison data. By including all these ideas, we end up with a graph that looks like Figure 12.3.

This is a much fairer and less misleading representation of the violence data on this campus. Violence prevention programming personnel at this school may want to address the verbal harassment/threat situation among students. They may also want to break these data out by grade level, gender, and race to determine whether the majority of this behavior is being committed by a particular subpopulation or subgroup. That information will also help target programming.

Shock Value

Shock value is an important point to revisit. On the basis of the data from Cityville High School, it could actually and accurately be said, "We had five instances of weapons violence last year and eight this year, which

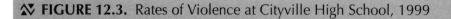

FIGURE 12.3. Rates of Violence at Cityville High School, 1999

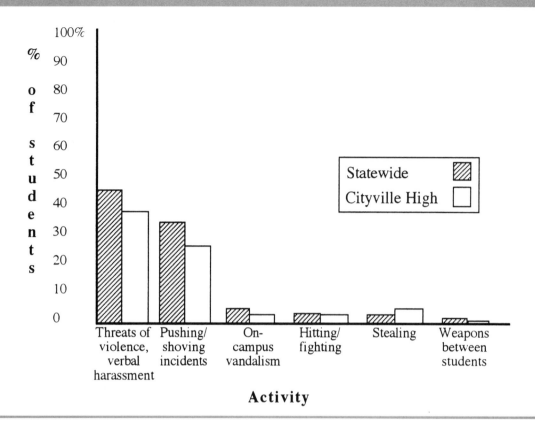

represents a 60% increase in weapons violence!" This statement is designed for shock value, not for accurate communication of behavior rates or trends. As previously mentioned, presenting data for shock value is often done to highlight a need for expanded programming, increased personnel, or additional funding. This is a dishonest way to present data, because it is intended to be deceptive. To present these data more accurately, they need to be converted from raw data into a percentage and then compared with baseline, local, state, or national rates and trends. As we saw in Figure 12.3, Cityville High School has lower rates of most types of violence than the rest of the schools in its state. School personnel may be able to attribute this fact to effective prevention programming.

To avoid having your data misrepresented, be selective in your release of raw data. Summarize your data into percentages, use measures of central tendency, and graph them with comparison data. Release these charts and graphs as part of your press release package.

Data Used Against Us

No matter what the annual program report says about your program's effectiveness, some persons will want it to say something else and will even reinterpret your best-made graph or chart to fit with their agenda. Below is a discussion of some common problems and responses that can be used.

To Delay or Postpone Decisions

"Do we really need to hire a prevention coordinator? Let's collect data for another year and see whether these numbers don't improve on their own, based on everyone now being more aware of the problem."

Response. Awareness will not expand prevention program delivery, the scope of the program, or the number of students receiving programming. If your data suggest that you need additional staff, then present the data that support that. Focus on the numbers of unserved students and the programming that did not get done because of lack of staffing.

As After-the-Fact Justification for Decisions Already Made

This heading may sound confusing unless you've been there. Imagine that, after you give your well-prepared presentation of your program results, someone with higher authority stands up and announces, "We have decided not to increase funding in our violence prevention program budget. These numbers seem to suggest that we're doing just fine without additional programming." The decision not to expand funding was made prior to your presentation; higher-ups are just using your data to justify themselves.

Response. Make sure your program results show that the student behavior change appears to be a result of involvement with your program. You'll need a good experimental design and some control group or comparison group data to do this. If your data can show that you need to expand programming but that you do not have the funds to do that, then present the data that show the numbers of unserved students and the programming that did not get done. Describe exactly what would be done with increased funds.

To Make a Poor Program Appear Legitimate

"As you can see, all our substance use rates are down over the past 3 years, so we'll be sticking with 'Wally the Magic Warthog' at the elementary level and 'The Flying Drug-Free Enchiladas' motivational assembly at the middle school."

Response. Make sure that your data are accurate and that you have adequate comparison data. Your use rates might be down, but with programs like these short-term or one-shot assemblies there's a good chance the reduction in your use rates has nothing to do with your programming. Use state and national data to show how use rates are down across the country, even in schools with no programming. Use data from neighboring communities to show that with effective programming, use rates could be much lower.

Bring in information about what elements need to be present for effective programming. Remind the audience about what type of prevention education is required by your state's education department. Bring in information about two or three effective programs, and describe their implementation and cost. Chances are that for the cost of The Flying Drug-Free Enchiladas assembly, you could train several teachers and buy class sets of more effective materials.

Interpreted to Suggest That Only Small Issues Need to Be Changed Rather Than Basic Approaches

"Our statistics show that bullying and teasing are beginning in fourth grade rather than fifth grade as we thought, so we'll just move the 'Scared Happy' guest speaker down one grade level."

Response. An ineffective program will be ineffective at any grade level. The basic approach to programming needs to be revisited. Introduce elements of effective prevention (see Chapter 4). Remind the audience that more than just a guest speaker is required for prevention programming by your own state's education department. Bring in two or three programs that have been proven effective, and describe their implementation and cost. Change is very threatening for some people. Offer small steps toward more effective programming.

Skewed to Smear Effective Programs That Are Threatening

"Teacher feedback on the program shows that they were out of their classrooms for training on four separate occasions, which is never good for students."

Response. The research is solid on the necessity of teacher training. Careful data will also be an important piece of this response. Show quantitatively that students who are participating in this program are doing better than students who are not. Use national data and local data. Show that these students were not hurt academically by their teachers being absent. Ask student participants to share their anecdotal experiences. Have teachers who have been implementing the program talk about their experiences. An effective program, when adequately measured, will sell itself.

▣ Conclusion

Be careful that you don't make yourself the messenger that everyone wants to shoot. You may be the first person who ever asked "Why are we doing this?" "Is this worth the time and money?" By asking those questions, you are dragging your school, agency, or community into the new millennium of prevention, a place where assessing outcomes is required and habit and complacency are suspect. No matter how resistant your administrator or community may be to the data you collect, you no longer have a choice. Whenever you present, it is a good idea to remind your audience that assessment of program outcomes is now required by most funders. This is now a necessary part of all program planning and won't be going away any time soon.

Your program's assessment may be the first of its kind ever to take place in your school community. Many people will welcome the information; many will fear and resist it. For some, it will mean finally being able to do worthwhile prevention. For others, it may mean the end of their jobs.

Remember to be sensitive to the power of the information you will discover. Keep in mind that the elementary prevention curriculum you just determined was useless may have been written by the superintendent's wife. The ineffective programs and people your data collection and assessment have identified may be beloved institutions in your prevention community. The results of program assessment can motivate you to move quickly, but lasting change takes time and patience. Seek the truth and tell the truth, but before all else, do no harm.

Second Thoughts ◀

▶ Never present data that do not tell the truth.

▶ Improve the accuracy and simplicity of data collection by standardizing the procedure.

▶ Don't panic if youth behavior doesn't improve or actually appears to worsen during the first year of programming.

▶ Make sure you are using proven programs or methods. It is much easier to defend your decision with empirical research for support.

▶ Write frequent and prosocial press releases.

▶ Include groups with agendas different from your own in the initial data review and program planning to minimize their opposition.

▶ Never present your data in a shock value format, no matter how much you need additional funds or staff. There is always an honest and equally compelling way to use your data to support program expansion.

▶ Be prepared to get blindsided by nonsupporters, often with your own data! If you stick to the facts, and if your facts and data are inarguably accurate, then you'll be the victor.

Principles of Effectiveness

The Principles of Effectiveness appeared in the June 1, 1998, *Federal Register.* These guidelines, or principles, govern the use of funding received under Title IV (Safe and Drug Free Schools and Communities Act). They became effective on July 1, 1998.

■ Principle 1

Conducting Needs Assessments

A grant recipient shall base its program on a thorough assessment of objective data about the drug and violence problems in the schools and communities served.

■ Principle 2

Setting Measurable Goals and Objectives

A grant recipient shall, with the assistance of a local or regional advisory council, which includes community representatives, establish a set of measurable goals and objectives, and design its activities to meet those goals and objectives.

■ Principle 3

Effective Research-Based Programs

A grant recipient shall design and implement its activities based on research or evaluation that provides evidence that the strategies used prevent or reduce drug use, violence, or disruptive behavior.

Principle 4 ■

Program Evaluation

A grant recipient shall evaluate its program periodically to assess its progress toward achieving its goals and objectives and use its evaluation results to refine, improve, and strengthen its program and to refine its goals and objectives as appropriate.

Resources for Evaluation

Andrews, F. M., Lem, L., Davidson, T. N., O'Malley, P., & Rodgers, W. L. (1978). *A guide for selecting statistical techniques for analyzing social science data.* Ann Arbor: University of Michigan, Institute for Social Research, Survey Research Center.

Carmona, C. S., Steward, K., Gottfredson, D. C., & Gottfredson, G. D. (1998). *A guide for evaluating prevention effectiveness, CSAP Technical Report* (NCADI Publication No. 98-3237). Rockville, MD: Center for Substance Abuse Prevention, Substance Abuse and Mental Health Services Administration.

CSAP Technical Report. (1998). *A guide for evaluating prevention effectiveness* (DHHS Publication No. 98-3237). Washington, DC: Center for Substance Abuse Prevention, National Center for the Advancement of Prevention.

French, J. F., & Kaufman, N. J. (Eds.). (1981). *Handbook for prevention evaluation: Prevention evaluation guidelines* (Publication No. ADM81-1145). Rockville, MD: National Institutes of Health, National Institute of Drug Abuse.

A guide for evaluating prevention effectiveness: Technical report. (1986). Washington, DC: U.S. Department of Health and Human Services, Substance Abuse and Mental Health Services Administration.

Hawkins, J. D., & Nederhood, B. (1987). *Handbook for evaluating drug and alcohol prevention programs: Staff/team evaluation of prevention programs* (Publication No. ADM 87-1512). Washington, DC: U.S. Department of Health and Human Services.

Heiman, G. W. (1992). *Basic statistics for the behavioral sciences.* Boston: Houghton Mifflin.

Isaac, S., & Michael, W. B. (1983). *Handbook in research and evaluation: A collection of principles, methods, and strategies useful in planning, designing, and evaluation of studies in education and the behavioral sciences* (2nd ed.). San Diego, CA: EdLTS Publishers.

Knowles, C. R. (2000). Taking the fear out of statistics. *Student Assistance Journal, 12*(2), 16-20.

Kozel, N. J., & Sloboda, Z. (1998). *Assessing drug abuse within and across communities: Community epidemiology surveillance networks on drug abuse* (NIH Publication No. 98-3614). Rockville, MD: National Institutes of Health, National Institute on Drug Abuse.

Larson, M. J., Buckley, J., & Gabriel, R. M. (1997). *A community substance abuse indicator's handbook: How do we know we are making a difference?* Boston: Join Together.

Miller, D. C. (1991). *Handbook of research design and social measurement* (5th ed.). Newbury Park, CA: Sage.

Moberg, D. P. (1984). *Evaluation of prevention programs: A basic guide for practitioners.* Madison: Board of Regents of the University of Wisconsin System for the Wisconsin Clearinghouse.

Muraskin, L. D. (1993). *Understanding evaluation: The way to better prevention programs* (Publication No. ED/OESE92-41). Washington, DC: U.S. Department of Education.

Myers, A. (1980). *Experimental psychology.* New York: Van Nostrand.

Sanders, J. R. (2000). *Evaluating school programs: An educator's guide* (2nd ed.). Thousand Oaks, CA: Corwin.

Thomas, S. J. (1999). *Designing surveys that work! A step-by-step guide.* Thousand Oaks, CA: Corwin.

Thompson, N. J., & McClintock, H. O. (1998). *Demonstrating your program's worth: A primer on evaluation for programs to prevent unintentional injury.* Atlanta, GA: Centers for Disease Control and Prevention, National Center for Injury Prevention and Control.

U.S. Department of Health and Human Services. (1987). *Handbook for evaluating drug and alcohol prevention programs* (Publication No. ADM87-1512). Washington, DC: Author.

U.S. Department of Health and Human Services. (1991). *Prevention plus III: Assessing alcohol and other drug prevention programs at the school and community level* (Publication No. ADM91-1817). Washington, DC: Author.

What, me evaluate? (1986). Washington, DC: National Crime Prevention Council.

W. K. Kellogg Foundation. (1998). *W. K. Kellogg Foundation evaluation handbook.* Battle Creek, MI: Collateral Management Company.

Additional On-Line Evaluation Resources ■

American Evaluation Association: www.eval.org

Electronic resources for evaluators. Available: www.luc.edu/faculty/eposava/resource.htm

A review of evaluation resources for nonprofit organizations. Available: www.ccp.ca/information/documents/gd44.htm

Practical evaluation of public health program workbook. Available: www.cdc.gov/phtn/catalog/vc0017.htm

University of Ottawa-Carleton Health Department program evaluation tool kit. Available: www.uottawa.ca/academic/med/epid/sld003.htm

■ Tools for the Evaluation of Web Sites

Emory University—Rollins School of Public Health: www.sph.emory.edu/WELLNESS/abstract.html

Indiana University: www.indiana.edu/~libresd/eval/review.htm

New York University: www.nyu.edu/education/hepr/resources/online/adq.pdf

Widener University: http://muse.widener.edu/Wolfgram-Memorial-Library/webevaluation/webeval.htm

Worksheet for Writing Measurable Objectives

Process Objectives

Process objectives are implementation objectives. How will you know that you were successful in implementing your program? Did you follow pre-scribed procedures, provide necessary training, stick to your purchasing budget, and complete all scheduled follow-up?

The four elements to a complete process objective are: When, How Much/How Many, Who, and What.

Step 1: Organize your language by using the following chart.

What	How Much/How Many	Who	Due Date

Step 2: Plug your language from the above grid into this sentence:

By _____*Date*_____, there will be _____*How Much/How Many*_____

_____*Who*_____ doing/finishing/presenting/trained in _____*What*_____.

Step 3: Now write them out as single sentence statements:

► _____

► _____

► _____

Outcome Objectives

When writing outcome objectives, the question you need to ask (and answer) is "What will these students look like *after* they have participated in this program?" Will they be better able to resolve conflict? Better able to control their tempers? Have more friends or lower smoking and drinking rates? Have better school attendance or improved grades?

The four key elements in a good outcome objective are (a) the behavior you would like to see changed, (b) the population you would like to see changed, (c) the percent of change you would like to see, and (d) the date by which you would like to accomplish this change. To make things easier, let's plug our language into a chart.

Step 1: Organize your language by using the following chart.

Behavior/Attitude	Population	% Change	When

Step 2: Plug your language from the above grid into this sentence:

_____*Behavior/Attitude*_____ among _____*Population*_____ will

_____*% Change*_____ by _____*When*_____ .

Step 3: Now write them out as single-sentence statements:

▶ _____

▶ _____

▶ _____

See Chapter 2 for more detail on problems and traps to avoid when writing objectives.

Program Timeline

Objective:				
Tasks	*Person Responsible*	*Resources*	*Due Date*	✔

Objective:				
Tasks	*Person Responsible*	*Resources*	*Due Date*	✔

Worksheet for Evaluating Web-Based Resources

Can you trust the accuracy of this Web site? Answer the following questions before you decide.

Site being reviewed: _____

1. **Purpose**

   a. What is the purpose or motivation for the site? _____

   _____

   b. Is the purpose for this site stated?   ❏ Yes   ❏ No

      ❏ educational site   ❏ unknown

      ❏ advertisement   ❏ other

      ❏ opinion exchange (If the information at this site is

      based on opinion, is this acknowledged?)   ❏ Yes   ❏ No

2. **Advertisements**

   a. Are there advertisements on the site?   ❏ Yes   ❏ No

   b. If so, are they clearly differentiated from
      the other content?   ❏ Yes   ❏ No

   c. Does the site have needed information,
      or is it just a pretty site?   ❏ needed   ❏ pretty

3. **Source**

   a. Who is the owner, author, or sponsor of the site? _____

   _____

b. What is the address and telephone number where she or he or they can be reached? _____

_____

c. Is the person/organization an authority for information in this field? ☐ Yes ☐ No

4. **Site Content**

a. Is the content accurate and objective? ☐ Yes ☐ No

b. Is the site content current? ☐ Yes ☐ No

c. How often is the site updated? _____

d. When was this specific page last revised? _____

e. Can you verify the content with two other sources of information? ☐ Yes ☐ No

f. Is the information grammatically and typographically accurate? ☐ Yes ☐ No
(Spelling, grammar, and typographical errors indicate a lack of quality control and can result in further inaccuracies when using the information.)

5. **Site Functioning**

a. Did you try the links? ☐ Yes ☐ No

b. Do they work? ☐ Yes ☐ No

c. Do they take you to relevant, interesting, and current places? ☐ Yes ☐ No

6. **Audience**

a. Who is the intended audience for this site? (This should be clearly stated at the site.) _____

b. Is the site appropriate for this age level? ☐ Yes ☐ No

7. **Recognition**

a. Has the site won any awards? ☐ Yes ☐ No

Resources for Research-Based or Science-Based Programs

Centers for Disease Control and Prevention (CDC)
Division of Violence Prevention
Mailstop K65
4770 Buford Highway, NE
Atlanta, GA 30341
770-488-1506
www.cdc.gov/ncipc/dvp/dvp.htm

Center for the Study and Prevention of Violence
Institute of Behavioral Science
University of Colorado at Boulder
Campus Box 442
Boulder, CO 80309-0442
303-492-8465
www.colorado.edu/cspv

Drug Strategies
1575 Eye Street, NW, Suite 210
Washington, DC 20005
202-289-9070
www.drugstrategies.org

National School Safety Center
141 Dusenberg Drive, Suite 11
Westlake Village, CA 91362
805-373-9977
www.nssc1.org

National Consortium on Violence Research (NCOVR)
Carnegie Mellon University
The Heinz School
5000 Forbes Avenue
Pittsburgh, PA 15213

412-268-8311
www.ncovr.heinz.cmu.edu

National Criminal Justice Reference Service (NCJRS)
P.O. Box 6000
Rockville, MD 20849-6000
800-851-3420
www.ncjrs.org

Center for the Prevention of School Violence
313 Chapanoke Road, Suite 140
Raleigh, NC 27603
800-299-6054
www.ncsu.edu/cpsv

U.S. Department of Education
Safe & Drug Free Schools Program
400 Maryland Avenue, SW
Washington, DC 20202
202-260-1856
www.ed.gov/offices/OESE/SDFS

U.S. Department of Justice
Office of Justice Programs
810 Seventh Street
Washington, DC 20001
202-307-5933
www.ojp.usdoj.gov

Substance Abuse and Violence Web Resources

AACAP (American Academy of Child & Adolescent Psychiatry) Facts for Families

> http://www.aacap.org/info_families/index.htm

About.com: Alcoholism

> http://www.alcoholism.about.com

Addiction Research Foundation

> http://www.arf.org/

Al-Anon/Alateen Family Group Headquarters, Inc.

> http://www.al-anon.alateen.org/

Al-Anon/Alateen World Service Office

> http://www.al-anon.org

Alcoholics Anonymous

> http://www.alcoholics-anonymous.org/

Alcoholism & Substance Abuse Providers of New York State

> http://www.asapnys.org

American Academy of Pediatrics

> http://www.aap.org/

American Arbitration Association

> http://www.adr.org

American Cancer Society, Tobacco & Cancer

> http://www.cancer.org/tobacco/

American Council for Drug Education
http://www.acde.org

American Drug and Alcohol Survey
http://www.rmbsi.com/index.html

American Heart Association
http://www.americanheart.org

American Law Enforcement Electronic Library
http://members.aol.com/deawatch

American Lung Association
http://www.lungusa.org/

American Medical Association, Adolescent Health On-Line
http://www.ama-assn.org/adolhlth/

American Public Health Association
http://www.apha.org/

American School Health Association
http://www.ashaweb.org/

Association of Cancer Online Resources
http://www.acor.org

Boys and Girls Clubs of America
http://www.bgca.org

Bureau for International Narcotics and Law Enforcement Affairs
http://www.state.gov/www/global/narcotics_law/

Bureau of Justice Statistics
http://www.ojp.usdoj.gov/bjs/

Camp Fire Boys and Girls
http://www.campfire.org

Campaign for Tobacco Free Kids
http://www.tobaccofreekids.org

**Central CAPT (Center for the Application of Prevention Technologies)
Effective Prevention Programs Database**
http://www.miph.org/capt/programs.html

CDC Division of Adolescent and School Health (DASH)
http://www.cdc.gov/nccdphp/dash/

CDC Division of Violence Prevention
http://www.cdc.gov/ncipc/dvp/dvp.htm

CDC Tobacco Information and Prevention Source (TIPS)
http://www.cdc.gov/tobacco/

Center for Effective Collaboration and Practice
http://www.air.org/cecp/

Center for Mental Health Services (CMHS)
http://www.samhsa.gov/centers/cmhs/cmhs.html

**Center for Mental Health Services (CMHS)
Knowledge Exchange Network (KEN)**
http://www.mentalhealth.org

Center for Positive Behavior Intervention and Support
http://www.stpreof.uoregon.edu

Center for Science in the Public Interest (Booze News)
http://www.cspinet.org/booze/index.html

Center for Substance Abuse Prevention
http://www.samhsa.gov/centers/csap/csap.html

Center for Substance Abuse Prevention, Grant Information
http://www.samhsa.gov/grants/grants.html

Center for the Prevention of School Violence
http://www.ncsu.edu/cpsv/

Center for the Study and Prevention of Violence (CSPV)
http://www.colorado.edu/cspv/

Centers for Disease Control and Prevention
http://www.cdc.gov

Child Welfare League of America
> http://www.cwla.org/

Coaches Playbook Against Drugs
> http://ojjdp.ncjrs.org/pubs/coachesplaybook/

Collaborative to Advance Social and Emotional Learning (CASEL)
> http://www.casel.org/

Common Sense, National PTA
> http://www.pta.org/commonsense

Community Anti-Drug Coalitions of America
> http://www.cadca.org

Community Policing Consortium
> http://www.communitypolicing.org

Conflict and Violence, Adolescence Directory On-Line
> http://www.education.indiana.edu/cas/adol/conflict.html

Creative Partnerships for Prevention
> http://www.cpprev.org

Crime Prevention Coalition of America
> http://www.crimepreventcoalition.org

Crime Stoppers International, Inc.
> http://www.c-s-i.org

Cybergrrl SafetyNet
> http://www.cybergrrl.com/fs.jhtml?/views/dv/index.shtml

Developmental Research and Programs
> http://www.drp.org/

Drug Enforcement Administration
> http://www.usdoj.gov/dea/

Drug Free Workplace
> http://www.drugfreeworkplace.com

Drug Reform Coordination Network
http://mir.drugtext.org/drcnet/

Drug Reform Coordination Network Online Library of Drug Policy
http://www.druglibrary.org/

DrugSense
http://www.drugsense.org

Drug Strategies
http://www.drugstrategies.org

Drug War Facts
http://www.drugwarfacts.org

Drugtext
http://www.drugtext.org/

Early Career Preventionists Network (ECPN)
http://www.oslc.org/Ecpn/intro.html

Environmental Protection Agency (EPA)
http://www.epa.gov

EthnoMedicinals for Research and Development
http://www.walden.mvp.net/~tonytork

Executive Office for Weed & Seed
http://www.ojp.usdoj.gov/eows

Federal Judicial Center
http://www.fjc.gov/

FedStats
http://www.fedstats.gov/

Fetal Alcohol Syndrome Information, Support & Communications Link
http://www.acbr.com/fas/

Food and Drug Administration
http://www.fda.gov

The Future of Children
http://www.futureofchildren.org/

Girls Incorporated
http://www.girlsinc.org

Go Ask Alice!
http://www.goaskalice.columbia.edu

Harm Reduction Coalition
http://www.harmreduction.org/

Harvard School of Public Health College Alcohol Study
http://www.hsph.harvard.edu/cas

Hate and Bias Crimes
http://www.ncjrs.org/hate_crimes/hate_crimes.html

Hazelden Foundation
http://www.hazelden.org/

Healthy Relationships Violence Prevention Curriculum
http://fox.nstn.ca/~healthy

Higher Education Center for Alcohol and Other Drug Prevention
http://www.edc.org/hec/

Illinois Alcoholism and Drug Dependence Association (IADDA)
http://www.iadda.org/

Indiana Prevention Resource Center
http://www.drugs.indiana.edu

Injury Control Resource Information Network
http://www.injurycontrol.com/icrin/

Institute on Violence and Destructive Behavior
http://www.uoregon.edu/~ivdb/

Johns Hopkins Prevention Research Center
http://mh.jhsph.edu/prevention_center.html

Join Together Online
http://www.jointogether.org/

Justice for Kids & Youth
http://www.usdoj.gov/kidspage

Keep Schools Safe
http://www.keepschoolssafe.org/

KidsPeace
http://www.kidspeace.org

Lindesmith Center—Drug Policy Foundation
http://www.lindesmith.org/

Marin Institute for the Prevention of Alcohol and Other Drug Problems
http://www.marininstitute.org/index.html

Monitoring the Future
http://www.monitoringthefuture.org/

Mothers Against Drunk Driving (MADD)
http://www.madd.org

Narcotics Anonymous
http://www.na.org/

National Alliance for Hispanic Health
http://www.hispanichealth.org

National Alliance for Safe Schools
http://www.safeschools.org

National Asian Pacific American Families Against Substance Abuse, Inc.
http://www.napafasa.org/

National Association for Children of Alcoholics
http://www.nacoa.net/

National Association for Community Mediation
http://www.nafcm.org

National Association for Native American Children of Alcoholics (NANACOA)
http://www.ael.org/eric/ned/ned019.htm

National Association of State Boards of Education
http://www.nasbe.org/

National Association of Teen Institutes
http://www.teeninstitute.org/

National Association of Town Watch, Inc.
http://www.nationaltownwatch.org

National Black Child Development Institute
http://www.nbcdi.org

National Center for Children in Poverty
http://cpmcnet.columbia.edu/dept/nccp/

National Center for Conflict Resolution Education
http://www.nccre.org

National Center for Health Statistics
http://www.cdc.gov/nchs/default.htm

National Center on Institutions and Alternatives
http://www.ncianet.org/ncia/

National Center for Missing and Exploited Children
http://www.missingkids.com/

National Center on Addiction and Substance Abuse at Columbia University
http://www.casacolumbia.org

National Clearinghouse for Alcohol and Drug Information
http://www.health.org

National Clearinghouse on Child Abuse and Neglect Information
http://www.calib.com/nccanch

National Coalition Against Domestic Violence
http://www.ncadv.org/

National Council on Alcoholism and Drug Dependence, Inc. (NCADD)
http://www.ncadd.org

National Crime Prevention Council
http://www.ncpc.org

National Criminal Justice Reference Service
http://www.ncjrs.org/

National Drug Strategies Network "NewsBriefs"
http://www.ndsn.org

National Drunk and Drugged Driving Prevention Month
http://www.3dmonth.org

National Education Association
http://www.nea.org/

National Educational Service
http://www.nes.org

National Families in Action
http://www.emory.edu/NFIA/

National Family Partnership
http://www.nfp.org/

National Head Start Association
http://www.nhsa.org

National Highway Traffic Safety Administration
http://www.nhtsa.dot.gov

National Household Survey on Drug Abuse
http://www.samhsa.gov/oas/p0000016.htm

National Inhalant Prevention Coalition
http://www.inhalants.org

National Institute on Alcohol Abuse and Alcoholism (NIAAA)
http://www.niaaa.nih.gov/

National Institute on Drug Abuse (NIDA)
http://www.nida.nih.gov/

National Institutes of Health
http://www.nih.gov/

National Institute of Mental Health
http://www.nimh.nih.gov/

National Law-Related Education Resource Center
http://www.abanet.org/publiced/nlrc.html

National Library of Medicine
http://www.nlm.nih.gov/

National Longitudinal Study of Adolescent Health
http://www.cpc.unc.edu/projects/addhealth/addhealth_home.html

National Mental Health and Education Center
http://www.naspcenter.org/index2.html

National Middle School Association
http://www.nmsa.org/

National Network for Youth
http://www.nn4youth.org

National Network of Education Regional Laboratories
http://www.nwrel.org/national/index.html

National Organization for Victim Assistance
http://www.try-nova.org/

National Parent Information Network
http://www.npin.org/

National PTA
http://www.pta.org/

National SAFE KIDS Campaign
http://www.safekids.org

National Safety Council
http://www.nsc.org

National School Safety Center
http://www.nssc1.org

National Urban League, Inc.
http://www.nul.org

National Youth Anti-Drug Media Campaign
http://www.mediacampaign.org

National Youth Gang Center
http://www.iir.com/nygc

Nemours Foundation
http://nemours.org/

New York State Center for School Safety
http://www.mhrcc.org/scss/

New York State Office of Alcoholism and Substance Abuse Services
http://www.oasas.state.ny.us/home.htm

Non-Alcoholic Drinks & Food
http://www.alcoholismhelp.com/index/html/sgp87.html

Office for Civil Rights
http://www.ed.gov/offices/OCR/

Office of Dietary Supplements, National Institutes of Health
http://dietary-supplements.info.nih.gov/

Office of Educational Research & Improvement
http://www.ed.gov/offices/OERI/#OERI

Office of the Federal Register, National Archives and Records Administration
http://www.access.gpo.gov/nara/index.html

Office of Juvenile Justice and Delinquency Prevention
http://www.ojjdp.ncjrs.org/

Office of Minority Health
  http://www.omhrc.gov

Office of National Drug Control Policy (ONDCP)
  http://www.whitehousedrugpolicy.gov

Office of Special Education Programs
  http://www.ed.gov/offices/OSERS/OSEP/index.html

Oregon Social Learning Center
  http://www.oslc.org/

Parents Resource Institute for Drug Education (PRIDE)
  http://www.prideusa.org/

Partnerships Against Violence Network (Pavnet)
  http://www.pavnet.org

Partnership for a Drug Free America
  http://www.drugfreeamerica.org/

Partnership for Responsible Drug Information
  http://www.prdi.org/

Peaceful Intervention Program
  http://www.cjnetworks.com/~msconsult/

President's Crime Prevention Council
  http://www.ncjrs.org/ddspcpc1.htm

PreventingCrime.Org
  http://www.preventingcrime.org/

Prevention Program Evaluations, Office of National Drug Control Policy
  http://www.whitehousedrugpolicy.gov/prevent/progeval.html

Prevention Researcher
  http://www.tpronline.org/index.cfm

Prevention Through Service Alliance
  http://www.ptsa.net/

Protective Schools

http://www.drugstats.org/prosch.html

ProvenEffective.com

http://www.proveneffective.com

RAND Drug Policy Research Center

http://www.rand.org/multi/oldrc/

Reality Check

http://www.health.org/reality/

Regional Resource and Federal Centers (RRFC) Network

http://www.dssc.org/frc/rrfc.htm

Research Triangle Institute

http://www.rti.org

Safe & Drug Free Schools Program

http://www.ed.gov/offices/OESE/SDFS

School Mental Health Project/Center for Mental Health in Schools (UCLA)

http://smhp.psych.ucla.edu/

Search Institute

http://www.search-institute.org/

Sentencing Project

http://www.sentencingproject.org/

Social Development Research Group

http://depts.washington.edu/sdrg/

Society for Prevention Research

http://www.oslc.org/spr/sprhome.html

StopHazing.org

http://www.stophazing.org

Stop the Violence

http://www.stv.net/main.htm

Student Pledge Against Gun Violence
http://www.pledge.org/

Students Against Driving Drunk
http://www.nat-sadd.org

Substance Abuse & Mental Health Services Administration
http://www.samhsa.gov/

Teen Deaths Due to Guns
http://ist-socrates.berkeley.edu:3333/faststats/teengundeaths.html

THOMAS Legislative Information on the Internet
http://thomas.loc.gov/

Tobacco Education & Prevention Program
http://www.tepp.org

Treatment Accountability for Safer Communities
http://www.ncjrs.org/txtfiles/tasc.txt

United States Institute of Peace
http://www.usip.org

U.S. Department of Health & Human Services
http://www.os.dhhs.gov

U.S. Department of Labor's Working Partners for an Alcohol- and Drug-Free Workplace
http://www.dol.gov/dol/workingpartners.htm

Virgina Youth Violence Project
http://curry.edschool.virginia.edu/curry/centers/youthvio/

Wisconsin Clearinghouse for Prevention Resources
http://www.uhs.wisc.edu/wch

Women, Infants and Children (WIC) Supplemental Nutrition Program
http://www.ventura.org/hca/dos/ph/dos_ph46.htm

World Drug Report
http://www.undcp.org/world_drug_report.html

World of Prevention Texas Youth Commission
http://www.tyc.state.tx.us/prevention/

YMCA of the USA
http://www.ymca.net

Youth Power Online
http://www.osom.org/youthpower/

Youth Violence: A Report of the Surgeon General
http://www.surgeongeneral.gov/library/youthviolence/

YWCA of the USA, Headquarters
http://www.ywca.org

Sample Youth Participant Feedback Sheet

Name of Program _____ Date _____

Answer the following questions as honestly as you can. Base your answers on what you personally think and feel. This sheet is anonymous; no one will know what you have written. If you have any questions, concerns, or suggestions about this program, talk with one of the leaders. Your honest feedback is important and will determine how we change and improve this program for future students.

	NO				YES
1. Is this room comfortable?	1	2	3	4	5
2. Do you think the materials are helpful to you?	1	2	3	4	5

Why or why not?_____

_____

3. Are these leaders effective in running this program?	1	2	3	4	5

Why or why not?_____

_____

4. What could be added to this program to make it better?

_____

_____

(continued)

5. What should we think about removing and WHY?

_____

_____

	NO				YES
6. Has this program made you consider things you hadn't really thought about before?	1	2	3	4	5
7. On the basis of your experience in this program, have you changed how you interact with your friends or family?	1	2	3	4	5

8. What else do we need to know?

_____

_____

Thank You!

Sample Adult Participant Feedback Sheet

Title of Workshop or Program: _____

Your position/job title: _____

Answer the following questions on the basis of your experience in this workshop or training experience. This feedback will be used to improve future programs of this type.

	Strongly Disagree			_Strongly Agree_	
1. The purpose of this training was clear.	1	2	3	4	5
2. The content of this training was appropriate.	1	2	3	4	5
3. I acquired useful information and strategies to use after this training.	1	2	3	4	5
4. Sufficient interaction occurred between the participants and the trainer.	1	2	3	4	5
5. The training environment was supportive to raising sensitive issues/questions.	1	2	3	4	5
6. There was sufficient opportunity for questions.	1	2	3	4	5
7. The audiovisual aids were appropriate and helpful.	1	2	3	4	5
8. This training met my individual needs and concerns.	1	2	3	4	5
9. The presenter was knowledgeable about this material.	1	2	3	4	5
10. The presentation was well prepared/organized.	1	2	3	4	5

(continued)

I liked: _____

_____

_____

I would change: _____

_____

_____

I still need: _____

_____

_____

Thank You!

Sample Classroom Observation Sheet*

Implementation Observation of Program _____

School _____ Teacher _____ Date _____

Class Period (time) _____ Grade Level _____ Number of students in class _____

Topic of lesson _____ Advertising _____

To what extent was the following information covered during this lesson:

	Not Covered		Covered		Completely Covered
1. Discussion of the function of advertising	1	2	3	4	5
2. Discussion of the extent of advertising	1	2	3	4	5
3. Discussion of cost of different types of advertising	1	2	3	4	5
4. Examination of six advertising techniques:					
a. Facts and figures	1	2	3	4	5
b. Sex appeal	1	2	3	4	5
c. Plain folks	1	2	3	4	5
d. Sensual	1	2	3	4	5
e. Bandwagon	1	2	3	4	5
f. Humor	1	2	3	4	5
5. Use of magazines to select print ads	1	2	3	4	5

(continued)

	Not Covered		Covered		Completely Covered
6. Use of worksheet Analyzing Ads	1	2	3	4	5
7. Discussion of accuracy of ads	1	2	3	4	5
8. Discussion of the misleading nature of tobacco and alcohol ads	1	2	3	4	5
9. Assignment: Developing counter ads	1	2	3	4	5

10. Estimate the percentage of time spent using the following teaching techniques

_____ % Lecture   _____ % Demonstration

_____ % Discussion   _____ % Practice

_____ % Small group work   _____ % Student presentation

11. How much time did this lesson take?   _____ minutes.

12. How well did students engage in or enjoy this lesson?   0   1   2   3   4   5

Comments:

_____

_____

_____

_____

_____

_____

_____

_____

_____

* Before observing a class, the observer should have an outline of the lesson or lesson plan to be taught. The Classroom Observation sheet should be developed partially on the basis of the lesson content. The goal with classroom observation is to ensure that this same lesson is implemented in the same way across all teachers and classes.

Sample Teacher Implementation Log

Name of Program _____ Date _____

Lesson # or Topic: _____

Teacher: _____

	NO				*YES*
1. I was able to complete material in this lesson in the prescribed time.	1	2	3	4	5
2. I was comfortable with the material in this lesson.	1	2	3	4	5
3. I felt rushed and reduced time in some areas in order to get everything covered.	1	2	3	4	5

4. Specifically, I reduced time on the following elements:

   _____

   _____

   _____

5. I needed to skip entirely the following elements:

   _____

   _____

   _____

(continued)

6. I made the following changes to this lesson (including additions):

_____

_____

_____

7. I would recommend the following minor changes:

_____

_____

_____

Sample En-Route Participant Feedback

Take a moment to provide the following feedback. This information will be used to improve this program.

	Low				*High*
1. Is this program what you expected it would be?	1	2	3	4	5
2. Do you think you are getting something out of your participation?	1	2	3	4	5
3. Is the room comfortable?	1	2	3	4	5
4. Are the materials helpful?	1	2	3	4	5
5. Are the materials and program content the right level for this age-group?	1	2	3	4	5
6. Are the program facilitators effective?	1	2	3	4	5

7. What else do we need to know? (For example, is there a better time of day or time of the week for us to do this program?)

8. What would improve the experience of future participants in this program?

Thank You!

RESOURCE M

On-line Federal Documents

Addiction Technology Transfer Centers (ATTC)
http://www.nattc.org

After-School Programs: Keeping Children Safe and Smart
http://www.ed.gov/pubs/afterschool/

Annual Report on School Safety, 1998
http://www.ed.gov/pubs/AnnSchoolRept98

Assessing Drug Abuse Within and Across Communities: Community Epidemiology Surveillance Networks on Drug Abuse
http://www.nida.nih.gov/DEPR/Assessing/Guideindex.html

Child Development/Community Policing: Partnership in a Climate of Violence
http://www.ncjrs.org/txtfiles/164380.txt

Combating Fear and Restoring Safety in Schools
http://www.ojjdp.ncjrs.org/jjbulletin/9804/contents.html

Conflict Resolution Education: A Guide to Implementing Programs in Schools, Youth-Serving Organizations, and Community and Juvenile Justice Settings
http://www.ncjrs.org/txtfiles/160935.txt

Creating Safe and Drug-Free Schools: An Action Guide
http://www.ed.gov/offices/OESE/SDFS/actguid/index.html

Early Warning, Timely Response: A Guide to Safe Schools
http://www.ed.gov/offices/OSERS/OSEP/earlywrn.html

Indicators of School Crime and Safety, 2000
http://www.nces.ed.gov/pubsearch/pubsinfo.asp?pubid-2001017

Juvenile Offenders and Victims: 1999 National Report
   http://www.ncjrs.org/html/ojjdp/nationalreport99/toc.html

Keeping Young People in School: Community Programs that Work
   http://www.ncjrs.org/txtfiles/dropout.txt

Kids and Guns
   http//:www.ncjrs.org/html/ojjdp/jjbul2000_03_2/contents.html

Manual to Combat Truancy
   http://www.ed.gov/pubs/Truancy

Mentoring—A Proven Delinquency Prevention Strategy
   http://www.ncjrs.org/txtfiles/164834.txt

Preventing Crime: What Works, What Doesn't, What's Promising
   http://www.preventingcrime.org/report/

Promising Strategies to Reduce Gun Violence
   http://ojjdp.ncjrs.org/pubs/gun_violence/contents.html

Reaching Out to Youth Out of the Mainstream
   http://www.ncjrs.org/txtfiles/163920.txt

Safe, Drug-Free, and Effective Schools for ALL Students: What Works!
   http://www.air.org/cecp/resources/safe&drug_free/main.htm

Safeguarding Our Children: An Action Guide
   http://www.ed.gov/offices/OSERS/OSEP/ActionGuide/

School House Hype: School Shootings and the Real Risks Kids Face in America
   http://www.cjcj.org/jpi/schoolhouse.html

Self-Reported Delinquency by 12-Year Olds
   http://ojjdp.ncjrs.org/about/00juvjust/000322b.html

Sharing Information: A Guide to the Family Educational Rights and Privacy Act and Participation in Juvenile Justice Programs
   http://www.ed.gov/offices/OM/findex.html

Truancy: First Step to a Lifetime of Problems
   http://ojjdp.ncjrs.org/about/97juvjust/jjtruncy.htm

W. K. Kellogg Foundation Evaluation Handbook
http://www.wkkf.org/Documents/WKKF/EvaluationHandbook/default.asp

"listservs" for Educators, Prevention Workers, and Other Service Providers

A *listserv* is an electronic newsletter or discussion group. Follow the directions, and each of these will bring current information about violence and substance abuse prevention directly to you via e-mail.

Who: **Criminal Justice News**
What: News in criminal justice, offers free publications
Where: www.listproc@ncjrs.org
How: In message field type: SUBSCRIBE JUSTINFO

Who: **Juvenile Justice News**
What: News in the juvenile justice system, offers free publications
Where: www.listproc@ncjrs.org
How: In message field type: SUBSCRIBE JUVJUST and your name

Who: **Join Together Online**
What: Substance-related news items from headlines
Where: www.jointogether.org
How: Click SUBSCRIBE button under "JTO Direct"

Who: **National Institute on Drug Abuse**
What: Effects of drug abuse on brain and behavior
Where: www.AnnounceNIDA@lists.nida.nih.gov
How: In subject field type SUBSCRIBE

Who: **Higher Education**
What: Substance-abuse prevention
Where: www.majordomo@mail.edc.org
How: In message field type: SUBSCRIBE HECNEWS-DIGEST

Who:	**Manisses Communications Group, Inc.**
Who:	**Manisses Communications Group, Inc.**
What:	Information on addiction, mental health, and children's services fields
Where:	www.manisses.com
How:	Fill in e-mail address and click the JOIN LIST button

Precursors to Substance Abuse and Violence

Individual Characteristics ■

► Impulsiveness, low self-control, hyperactivity, concentration problems, restlessness, and risk taking

► Poor social competency skills (inability to identify likely consequences of behavior, inability to find solutions to problems, no empathy and poor interpretation of social cues)

► Association with or exposure to negative peers

► Peer rejection

► Early and persistent antisocial behavior as seen by violation of school rules, violent behavior, poor attendance, substance abuse, teen pregnancy, vandalism, dropping out

► Beliefs and attitudes favorable to deviant or antisocial behavior

► Aggressiveness, early initiation of violent behavior

School-Classroom Environment ■

► Academic failure in elementary school, poor attendance

► Lack of commitment to school, little or no involvement in school life, no participation in extracurricular activities, special clubs, or events offered through the school

► Low bonding to school: truancy, dropping out

► Availability of drugs, alcohol, and weapons

► Weak academic mission

► Poor communication of rules, expectations, and consequences or inconsistent enforcement of rules and consequences

- ► Policies, regulations, and procedures inadequate to manage aggression and violence

- ► Lack of administrative leadership

- ► Poor climate of emotional support

- ► Frequent school transitions

■ Family Influence

- ► Parental substance abuse or criminality, or attitudes favorable to substance abuse or criminality

- ► Child maltreatment

- ► Poor family management practices, family conflict

- ► Low levels of parental involvement, poor family bonding

- ► Parent-child separation

■ Peer Influence

- ► Substance abusing or delinquent siblings

- ► Substance abusing or delinquent peers

- ► Gang membership

■ Community Influence

- ► Poverty

- ► Community disorganization

- ► Availability of drugs or firearms

- ► Neighborhood adults involved with substance abuse or crime

- ► Exposure to violence and racial prejudice

*　*　*　*　*

Gottfredson, D. C., Sealock, M. D., & Koper, C. S. (1996). Delinquency. In R. DiClemente, W. Hansen, & L. Ponton (Eds.), *Handbook of adolescent health risk behavior.* New York: Plenum.

Hawkins, J. D., Herrenkohl, T. I., Farrington, D. P., Brewer, D., Catalano, R. F., Harachi, T. W., & Cothern, L. (2000). *Predictors of youth violence* (Juvenile Justice Bulletin #179065). Washington, DC: Office of Juvenile Justice and Delinquency Prevention.

Effective Teaching and Organizational Methods

How the micro-environments of the classroom and school are managed and organized can directly affect the disorderly behavior of students. School and classroom organization are also important precursors of delinquency and drug use.

Instructional Interventions ■

- ▶ Cooperative learning techniques
- ▶ Experiential learning
- ▶ Continuous progress instruction (invariant sequence, testing for mastery at each level)
- ▶ Tutoring
- ▶ Computer-assisted instruction
- ▶ Clearly articulated expectations and rules
- ▶ Classroom organization and management techniques that promote ease of enforcement of classroom rules
- ▶ Behavioral techniques for classroom management; use of rewards and punishments
- ▶ Management of time to reduce "downtime"
- ▶ Strategies for grouping students within the classroom
- ▶ Use of external resources such as parent volunteers

Schoolwide Intervention ■

- ▶ Decreased class size, specifically in kindergarten and first grade
- ▶ Formation of grade level "houses" or "teams"

▶ Tracking into classes by ability, effort, achievement

▶ Nongraded elementary schools

* * * * *

Brewer, D. D., Hawkins, J. D., Catalano, R. F., & Neckerman, H. J. (1995). Preventing serious, violent, and chronic juvenile offending: A review of evaluations of selected strategies in childhood, adolescence, and the community. In J. C. Howell, B. Krisberg, J. D. Hawkins, & J. J. Wilson (Eds.), *Serious, violent, and chronic juvenile offenders: A source book.* Thousand Oaks, CA: Sage.

Sources of National Youth Data:
Substance Abuse and Violence — Rates and Trends

American Drug and Alcohol Survey
http://www.rmbsi.com/index.html

Bureau of Justice Statistics
http://www.ojp.usdoj.gov/bjs/

Census Data
http://www.census.gov/

Centers for Disease Control and Prevention (CDC)
http://www.cdc.com/

Centers for Disease Control and Prevention, Division of Adolescent and School Health (DASH)
http://www.cdc.gov/nccdphp/dash

Centers for Disease Control and Prevention, Division of Violence Prevention
http://www.cdc.gov/ncipc/dvp/dvp.htm

Center for Mental Health Services
http://www.samhsa.gov/cmhs

Center for Substance Abuse Prevention
http://www.samhsa.gov/csap/index.htm

Community Anti-Drug Coalitions of America
http://www.cadca.org

Community Oriented Policing Services (COPS)

http://www.usdoj.gov/cops

Facts About Gun Violence

http://www.aacap.org/info_families/NationalFacts/coGunViol.htm

FedStats

http://www.fedstats.gov/

Monitoring the Future Study

http://monitoringthefuture.org/

National Crime Victimization Survey, 1995

http://www.ojp.usdoj.gov/bjs/abstract/ncvs95p.htm

National Criminal Justice Reference Service (NCJRS)

http://www.ncjrs.org

National Highway Traffic Safety Administration

http://www.nhtsa.dot.gov

National Household Education Survey (NHES)

http://www.wisc.edu/dpls.cat/study/3605.html

National Household Survey on Drug Abuse

http://www.samhsa.gov/oas/nhsda/pe1996/httoc.htm

National Institute on Alcohol Abuse and Alcoholism (NIAAA)

http://www.niaaa.nih.gov

National Institute on Drug Abuse

http://www.nida.nih.gov

National Institute of Justice

http://www.ojp.usdoj.gov/nij

National Institute of Mental Health

http://www.nimh.nih.gov

Office of Special Education Programs

http://www.ed.gov/offices/OSERS/OSEP

Offices of Correctional Education
    http://www.ed.gov/offices/OVAE/OCE

Office of Juvenile Justice and Delinquency Prevention (OJJDP)
    http://www.ojjdp.ncjrs.org

Partnership for a Drug Free America
    http://www.drugfreeamerica.org/

Regional Education Laboratories
    http://www.nwrel.org/national/

Research Triangle Institute
    http://www.rti.org

School Crime Supplement to the National Crime Victimization Survey (SCS)
    http://www.ojp.usdoj.gov/bjs/pub/ascii/srsc.txt

Schools and Staffing Survey (SASS)
    http://www.nces.ed.gov/surveys/sass/

Substance Abuse & Mental Health Services Administration (SAMHSA)
    http://www.samhsa.gov

Teen Deaths Due to Guns
    http://ist-socrates.berkeley.edu:3333/faststats/teengundeaths.html

U.S. Department of Education
    http://www.ed.gov

U.S. Department of Health and Human Services
    http://www.os.dhhs.gov

U.S. Department of Justice
    http://www.usdoj.gov

Violence and Discipline Progems in U.S. Public Schools: 1996-97
    http://nces.ed.gov/pubs98/violence/index.html

Youth Risk Behavior Survey (1999)
    http://www.cdc.gov/nccdphp/dash/yrbs/survey99.htm

RESOURCE R

Where to Find Student Surveys on Substance Use and Other Risk Behaviors

American Drug and Alcohol Survey
Rocky Mountain Behavioral Science Institute
419 Canyon Avenue, Suite 316
Fort Collins, CO 80521
800-447-6354
www.rmbsi.com/drug_survey.html

Center fo Alcohol and Other Drug Studies
Student Health Programs
Southern Illinois University at Carbondale
Carbondale, IL 62901
618-453-4366
www.siu.edu/departments/coreinst/public_html/newsurvey.html

Harris Interactive
Survey Research for Education
135 Corporate Woods
Rochester, NY 14623
800-866-7655
www.harrisinteractive.com

PRIDE Surveys
166 St. Charles Street
Bowling Green, KY 42101
800-279-6361
www.pridesurveys.com/

Respect & Protect: Staff and Student Survey
(violence prevention and intervention)
Johnson Institute
152151 Pleasant Valley Road
P.O. Box 176
Center City, MN 55012-0176
800-328-9000

StudentView Survey
Johnson Institute
152151 Pleasant Valley Road
P.O. Box 176
Center City, MN 55012-0176
800-328-9000

Survey of Student Resources and Assets
Search Institute/America's Promise
700 South Third Street, Suite 210
Minneapolis, MN 55415
800-888-7828
www.search-institute.org/surveys/

Sample Teacher Survey of Curriculum Content: Violence Prevention

Take a moment to answer the following questions as accurately as you can. You do not have to dedicate an entire class period to any of these topics in order to respond positively that you have covered them. Sometimes these are simply "teachable moments" and happen briefly.

During the previous school year, did you . . .

	Never				*Often*
1. Teach students that people can have two different perspectives of the same event?	1	2	3	4	5
2. Teach how anger can escalate and model techniques to control it?	1	2	3	4	5
3. Teach negotiation skills?	1	2	3	4	5
4. Teach media awareness:					
a. How the media can glamorize the use of alcohol, tobacco, and other drugs?	1	2	3	4	5
b. How the media glorify and normalize violence?	1	2	3	4	5
5. Teach skills for handling provocative situations like teasing, bullying, and harassment?	1	2	3	4	5
6. Teach active listening skills?	1	2	3	4	5

	Never				*Often*
7. Teach students how to make and maintain friendships?	1	2	3	4	5
8. Discuss diversity or any topic that touched on cultural sensitivity?	1	2	3	4	5
9. Use more interactive teaching techniques such as group work, cooperative learning, and practice of skills?	1	2	3	4	5
10. Have you adapted any materials for work with a particular group of students?	1	2	3	4	5

11. Estimate how many class periods you devoted this year to these types of lessons.   _____ Class periods

12. Have you attended any teacher training on violence or substance abuse prevention?   ❒ No   ❒ Yes ____ Hours

Thank You!

Sample Teacher Survey of Curriculum Content: Substance Abuse Prevention

Take a moment to answer the following questions as accurately as you can. You do not have to dedicate an entire class period to any of these topics in order to respond positively that you have covered them. Sometimes these are simply "teachable moments" and happen briefly.

During the previous school year, did you . . .

	Never				*Often*
1. Teach students that the use of alcohol and drugs is unhealthy and unsafe (rather than "bad" or "wrong")?	1	2	3	4	5
2. Teach that people who choose to use alcohol or drugs may be making unhealthy and unsafe choices but aren't bad people?	1	2	3	4	5
3. Teach assessment of personal risk factors?	1	2	3	4	5
4. Teach media awareness:					
a. How the media can glamorize the use of alcohol, tobacco, and other drugs?	1	2	3	4	5
b. How the media glorify and normalize drug and alcohol use?	1	2	3	4	5
5. Teach skills for handling difficult situations in which students might be offered drugs or alcohol?	1	2	3	4	5

	Never				*Often*
6. Provide time for practice of new skills?	1	2	3	4	5
7. Provide incentives for low-risk choices?	1	2	3	4	5
8. Correct perceptions of peer use behaviors?	1	2	3	4	5
9. Integrate information about substance abuse prevention into other subject areas?	1	2	3	4	5
10. Have you adapted any materials for work with a particular group of students?	1	2	3	4	5

11. Estimate how many class periods you devoted this year to these types of lessons. _____ Class periods

12. Have you attended any teacher training on substance abuse prevention? ❏ No ❏ Yes ____ Hours

Thank You!

Data Summary Log*

1. Our community is: ☐ Rural ☐ Suburban ☐ Urban

2. The total number of youth represented by these data is: $N =$ _____

3. Youth data broken out by age:

   _____ 8 or younger _____ 11 _____ 14 _____ 17

   _____ 9 _____ 12 _____ 15 _____ 18

   _____ 10 _____ 13 _____ 16 _____ over 18

4. Youth data broken out by sex:

   _____ # Males _____ % Male

   _____ # Females _____ % Female

5. Youth data broken out by race:

   _____ African American

   _____ American Indian

   _____ Asian or Pacific Islander

   _____ Hispanic

   _____ Caucasian (white)

   _____ Other

6. Do your data represent a random sample of the general population of youth in your community?

   ☐ Yes ☐ No

If you answered YES to Question 6, proceed to the following questions.
If you answered NO to Question 6, collect further data before continuing.

* * * * *

7. At what age does tobacco use begin? _____

8. At what age does tobacco use peak? _____

9. Are there significant disparities between sexes
   and/or races with regard to tobacco use?
   ❒ No ❒ Yes Describe: _____

10. At what age does alcohol use begin? _____

11. At what age does alcohol use peak? _____

12. Are there significant disparities between sexes and/or races
    with regard to alcohol use?
    ❒ No ❒ Yes Describe: _____

13. At what age does marijuana use begin? _____

14. At what age does marijuana use peak? _____

15. Are there significant disparities between sexes and/or races
    with regard to marijuana use?
    ❒ No ❒ Yes Describe: _____

16. At what age does other drug use begin? _____

17. At what age does other drug use peak? _____

18. Are there significant disparities between sexes and/or races
    with regard to other drug use?
    ❒ No ❒ Yes Describe: _____

19. How harmful do students perceive the occasional or regular use
    of tobacco, alcohol, and other drugs?

	% finding occasional use harmful	*% finding regular use harmful*
Tobacco	_____	_____
Alcohol	_____	_____
Marijuana	_____	_____
Other drugs	_____	_____

20. At what age does bullying behavior begin? _____

21. At what age does bullying behavior peak? _____

(continued)

22. Are there significant disparities between sexes and/or races with regard to bullying behavior?
    ☐ No   ☐ Yes   Describe: _____

23. At what age do prejudice, bias, and intolerance begin?   _____

24. At what age do prejudice, bias, and intolerance peak?   _____

25. Are there significant disparities between sexes and/or races with regard to prejudice, bias, and intolerance?
    ☐ No   ☐ Yes   Describe: _____

26. At what age does hitting or physical fighting begin?   _____

27. At what age does hitting or physical fighting peak?   _____

28. Are there significant disparities between sexes and/or races with regard to hitting or physical fighting?
    ☐ No   ☐ Yes   Describe: _____

29. At what age does weapon possession begin?   _____

30. At what age does weapon possession peak?   _____

31. Are there significant disparities between sexes and/or races with regard to weapon possession?
    ☐ No   ☐ Yes   Describe: _____

32. Where is bullying most likely to take place?
    ☐ bus   ☐ halls   ☐ cafeteria
    ☐ bathrooms   ☐ classrooms   ☐ athletic fields
    ☐ locker rooms   ☐ other

33. At what age does criminal behavior begin?   _____

34. At what age does criminal behavior peak?   _____

35. Are there significant disparities between sexes and/or races with regard to criminal behavior?
    ☐ No   ☐ Yes   Describe: _____

36. What are the most common crimes being committed by school-age youth?

    1st _____

    2nd _____

    3rd _____

37. Compared with state or national statistics, our school community rates are:

Tobacco use, last 30 days	❑ Lower	❑ Same	❑ Higher
Alcohol use, last 30 days	❑ Lower	❑ Same	❑ Higher
Marijuana use, last 30 days	❑ Lower	❑ Same	❑ Higher
Other drug use, last 30 days	❑ Lower	❑ Same	❑ Higher
Tobacco use, past year	❑ Lower	❑ Same	❑ Higher
Alcohol use, past year	❑ Lower	❑ Same	❑ Higher
Marijuana use, past year	❑ Lower	❑ Same	❑ Higher
Other drug use, past year	❑ Lower	❑ Same	❑ Higher
Bullying behaviors	❑ Lower	❑ Same	❑ Higher
Sexual harassment	❑ Lower	❑ Same	❑ Higher
Prejudice, bias, and intolerance	❑ Lower	❑ Same	❑ Higher
Hitting or physical fighting	❑ Lower	❑ Same	❑ Higher
Weapon possession	❑ Lower	❑ Same	❑ Higher
Juvenile arrests	❑ Lower	❑ Same	❑ Higher

*Depending on what issues your school community is working on, add to this log as necessary. Are you concerned with smoking in bathrooms? Discrimination on sport teams? Add those data to this log!

Sample Student Risk Survey

(This sample is incomplete and not intended for use as is. It has never been tested for reliability or validity. It is provided here as an example of how to write survey items and what types of information might be relevant to prevention programming. A more complete survey might include questions about other risk behaviors, protective factors, and additional areas of health and safety.)

1. The grade you will be completing this year.
   - ☐ 7th
   - ☐ 8th
   - ☐ 9th
   - ☐ 10th
   - ☐ 11th
   - ☐ 12th

2. What is your age?
   - ☐ 11
   - ☐ 12
   - ☐ 13
   - ☐ 14
   - ☐ 15
   - ☐ 16
   - ☐ 17
   - ☐ 18
   - ☐ 19

3. What is your gender?
   - ☐ Male
   - ☐ Female

4. How do you describe yourself?
   - ☐ African American
   - ☐ American Indian
   - ☐ Asian or Pacific Islander (Cambodian, Hmong, Japanese, Korean, Laotian, Vietnamese)
   - ☐ Hispanic (Cuban, Mexican, Puerto Rican, other Latin American)
   - ☐ Caucasian (white)
   - ☐ other _____

5. How many times, if any, have you smoked cigarettes during the last
   30 days?

   ☐ 0   ☐ 6–9
   ☐ 1   ☐ 10–19
   ☐ 2   ☐ 20–39
   ☐ 3–5   ☐ 40+

6. How many times, if any, have you smoked cigarettes during the past
   12 months?

   ☐ 0   ☐ 6–9
   ☐ 1   ☐ 10–19
   ☐ 2   ☐ 20–39
   ☐ 3–5   ☐ 40+

7. How many times, if any, have you used alcohol during the past 30 days?

   ☐ 0   ☐ 6–9
   ☐ 1   ☐ 10–19
   ☐ 2   ☐ 20–39
   ☐ 3–5   ☐ 40+

8. How many times, if any, have you used alcohol during the past
   12 months?

   ☐ 0   ☐ 6–9
   ☐ 1   ☐ 10–19
   ☐ 2   ☐ 20–39
   ☐ 3–5   ☐ 40+

9. How many times, if any, have you used marijuana during the last
   30 days?

   ☐ 0   ☐ 6–9
   ☐ 1   ☐ 10–19
   ☐ 2   ☐ 20–39
   ☐ 3–5   ☐ 40+

10. How many times, if any, have you used marijuana during the past
    12 months?

    ☐ 0   ☐ 6–9
    ☐ 1   ☐ 10–19
    ☐ 2   ☐ 20–39
    ☐ 3–5   ☐ 40+

(continued)

||||➡ You may want to add questions that deal with a specific drug use problem in your district, like Ritalin, inhalants, or other substances that you have reason to suspect are popular.

11. In your circle of friends, how many would you say have done the following:

		None		*Some*		*All*
a. Drink alcohol once a week.		1	2	3	4	5
b. Use marijuana more than once a month.		1	2	3	4	5
c. Smoked cigarettes.		1	2	3	4	5
d. Have used other drugs, like speed or Ritalin.		1	2	3	4	5
e. Have used other drugs like cocaine or LSD.		1	2	3	4	5
f. Have been bullied or harassed by another student.		1	2	3	4	5
g. Have participated in bullying or harassing another student.		1	2	3	4	5
h. Have been in a physical fight.		1	2	3	4	5
i. Have been in trouble with the police.		1	2	3	4	5
j. Have carried a weapon to school.		1	2	3	4	5

12. Respond to the following statements, indicating how strongly you agree or disagree by circling the appropriate number from 1 to 5.

	Strongly Disagree				*Strongly Agree*
a. My school has clear rules about what happens if you are caught using tobacco products.	1	2	3	4	5
b. The rules about student alcohol and drug use are fair.	1	2	3	4	5
c. Students who violate alcohol and drug policies will receive immediate and consistent consequences.	1	2	3	4	5
d. I know where I can get a copy of my school's policy on student alcohol and drug use.	1	2	3	4	5

	Strongly *Disagree*			*Strongly* *Agree*	

e. My school's alcohol and drug policy is effective in helping students choose not to use. 1 2 3 4 5

f. It is wrong to bully or harass another student. 1 2 3 4 5

g. If I am caught harassing another student, I am sure to be punished. 1 2 3 4 5

h. Our district welcomes students from different cultures. 1 2 3 4 5

i. I have friends who are a different race than I am. 1 2 3 4 5

j. I have heard other students talking about fighting. 1 2 3 4 5

k. I have been involved in a physical fight. 1 2 3 4 5

l. I have seen weapons in my school. 1 2 3 4 5

m. I feel safe in school. 1 2 3 4 5

13. If you had a concern about someone harassing you, who would you talk to about it? (Mark all that apply to you.)

☐ No one   ☐ Neighbor

☐ Parent   ☐ Teacher

☐ Friend   ☐ Nurse/doctor

☐ Brother or sister   ☐ Coach

☐ Other relative   ☐ Other _____

14. If you had a concern about alcohol, tobacco, or other drugs, who would you talk to about it? (Mark all that apply to you.)

☐ No one   ☐ Neighbor

☐ Parent   ☐ Teacher

☐ Friend   ☐ Nurse/doctor

☐ Brother or sister   ☐ Coach

☐ Other relative   ☐ Other _____

(continued)

15. How safe do you think the following things would be for a person of your age?

		Not at All Dangerous				Very Dangerous
a.	Try tobacco once	1	2	3	4	5
b.	Smoke cigarettes 1 or 2 times a month	1	2	3	4	5
c.	Smoke cigarettes 1 or 2 times a day	1	2	3	4	5
d.	Smoke 5 to 10 cigarettes a day	1	2	3	4	5
e.	Try marijuana once	1	2	3	4	5
f.	Smoke marijuana 1 or 2 times a month	1	2	3	4	5
g.	Smoke marijuana daily	1	2	3	4	5
h.	Try alcohol once	1	2	3	4	5
i.	Drink alcohol 1 or 2 times a month	1	2	3	4	5
j.	Drink alcohol daily	1	2	3	4	5
k.	Drink until you are drunk once	1	2	3	4	5
l.	Drink until you are drunk every weekend	1	2	3	4	5
m.	Be a passenger in a car with a driver who has been drinking but who doesn't appear to be drunk	1	2	3	4	5
n.	Be a passenger in a car with a drunk driver	1	2	3	4	5

16. Have you ever been arrested?

❐ Yes   ❐ No

17. Have you ever been convicted of a crime (even as a JD)?

❐ vandalism   ❐ trespassing
❐ truancy   ❐ public disturbance
❐ shoplifting   ❐ breaking and entering
❐ fighting   ❐ car theft
❐ harassment/stalking ❐ possession
❐ sale of drugs   ❐ other

Sample Active Parent Consent Form

_____(name of school)_____ is taking part in the _(name of survey or program)_. Students in grades _(specify grade levels)_ will be surveyed to document their attitudes, behavior, and knowledge about _(indicate survey content here)_. This survey was developed/supported by _____(name of organization)_____.

Doing this pen-and-paper survey will not put your child at risk. This is an anonymous survey designed to protect your child's privacy. Students will not put their names on the surveys. No specific or identifying student information will ever be shared. Student names will never be used in reporting the results.

Although taking this survey will not be of immediate benefit to your child, all children will ultimately benefit from the results. The information collected from this survey will be used to guide the development and implementation of new programs in our school and community.

We would like all our students to participate in this survey. However, participation in this survey is voluntary. No action will be taken against you or your child if you decide not to participate.

Please read the tear-off section below, and check off one box indicating whether you do or do not want your child to participate in this survey. Return this form to the school by _____(date)_____.

See the other side of this form for more facts about the survey. If you have additional questions, please call _(contact person name and telephone)_.

Thank you!

------------✂------------------------------------

Child's name: _____ Grade: _____

I have read this form and know what the survey is about.

❏ My child *may* take part in this survey.

❏ My child *may not* take part in this survey.

Parent's signature: _____ Date: _____

Daytime telephone: _____

RESOURCE X

Sample Passive Parent Consent Form

_____(name of school)_____ is taking part in the _(name of survey or program)._ Students in grades _(specify grade levels)_ will be surveyed to document their attitudes, behavior, and knowledge about _(indicate survey content here)._ This survey was developed/supported by _____(name of organization)_____.

Doing this pen-and-paper survey will not put your child at risk. This is an anonymous survey designed to protect your child's privacy. Students will not put their names on the surveys. No specific or identifying student information will ever be shared. Student names will never be used in reporting the results.

Although taking this survey will not be of immediate benefit to your child, all children will ultimately benefit from the results. The information collected from this survey will be used to guide the development and implementation of new programs in our school and community.

We would like all our students to participate in this survey. However, participation in this survey is voluntary. No action will be taken against you or your child if you decide not to participate.

Please read the tear-off section below. You need only return this form if you do not want your child to participate in this survey.

See the other side of this form for more facts about the survey. If you have additional questions, please call _(contact person name and telephone)._

Thank you!

- - - - - ✄ -

Child's name: _____ Grade: _____

I have read this form and know what the survey is about.

❏ My child *may not* take part in this survey.

Parent's signature: _____ Date: _____

Daytime telephone: _____

Cost Effectiveness Worksheet

1. Personnel
   (Salaries, benefits, overtime, substitutes)   1. _____

2. Materials*
   *(Books, videos, computer software, folders and other paper
   products, pens/pencils, other office supplies or minor equipment)*   2. _____

3. Equipment
   *(Desks, chairs, VCRs, TVs, computers,
   file cabinets, coffee pots, copiers, fax machines)*   3. _____

4. Space
   (Rent, usage fees, heat, water)   4. _____

5. Purchased Services
   *(Service contracts, repair costs, equipment rentals, hotel rooms,
   telephone lines, janitorial or transportation services, tuition)*   5. _____

6. Miscellaneous
   *(All expenses not previously captured, food, travels,
   registration fees, subscriptions, memberships, tolls and parking.
   Some of these might fall under Purchased Services. Don't
   count them twice, but make sure they all get counted.)*   6. _____

7. Total (Gross Program Cost)   7. _____

8. Number of Students Directly Involved With This Program   8. _____
   (Nonduplicated count)

9. Total Cost per Student   9. _____
   *Divide your Gross Program Cost (line 7) by the total number
   of students (line 8).*

*Generally funders have rules about what is considered "equipment" and what is
considered a "supply." The cutoff is often $500 or $1000. Anything above that is
equipment, and anything below is a supply, regardless of what the item is. If you
are not sure, check with your business office or refer to the financial form or budget for this program.

Time Management Worksheet

Program A: _____ Program B: _____
Program C: _____ Program D: _____

Time	Activity	Program

Determining Percentage of ■
Time Worked per Program

To determine the percentage of time spent on each program, you will need to do some basic math. First, determine the total minutes worked during this period (week, month, semester), subtracting time spent at lunch. This will be a large number. Second, add up the minutes spent at each program and insert the totals into the worksheet below (see the example).

You do not have to figure these percentages in minute time units. You may use any unit of time as long as you are consistent throughout the calculations.

Follow these directions to arrive at the percentage of time worked for each program.

Example:

Total minutes worked – lunch = __9000__ (1 month)					
Program Minutes	÷ **Total minutes**	=	**ratio x 100**	=	**% time**
Program A: 4500	÷ 9000	=	.50 x 100	=	50%
Program B: 2100	÷ 9000	=	.23 x 100	=	23%
Program C: 1800	÷ 9000	=	.20 x 100	=	20%
Program D: 600	÷ 9000	=	.066 x 100	=	7%

Total minutes worked – lunch = _____					
Program Minutes	÷ **Total minutes**	=	**ratio x 100**	=	**% time**
Program A:	÷	=	x 100	=	
Program B:	÷	=	x 100	=	
Program C:	÷	=	x 100	=	
Program D:	÷	=	x 100	=	

Sample Youth Participant Pretest

Take a moment to answer the following questions. The first three questions will allow us to track your survey while you remain anonymous!

1. First three letters of your middle name ☐ ☐ ☐

2. First three letters of your mother's first name ☐ ☐ ☐

3. First three letters of the town where you were born ☐ ☐ ☐

4. Last two digits of the year in which you were born ☐ ☐

5. What is your ethnic background (use a two-letter code)? ☐ ☐
   WH - Caucasian (white)   NA - American Indian
   AA - African American   HA - Hispanic American
   AS - Asian; Pacific Islander   OT - Other

	Disagree		Not sure		Agree
6. I think the adults in my community value me.	1	2	3	4	5
7. I think I make useful and important contributions to my neighborhood or community.	1	2	3	4	5
8. Most of the time I am able to resist negative peer pressure and dangerous situations.	1	2	3	4	5
9. Overall, I'm glad I'm the person that I am.	1	2	3	4	5
10. I think through the possible negative and positive consequences before I make a decision.	1	2	3	4	5
11. The adults in my town listen to what I have to say.	1	2	3	4	5
12. Even if other people don't always agree, I will stand up for my beliefs and act on my convictions.	1	2	3	4	5

During the last 30 days, how often have you . . .

13.	Smoked tobacco?	0	1	2	3-5	6-9	10+
14.	Smoked marijuana?	0	1	2	3-5	6-9	10+
15.	Used alcohol?	0	1	2	3-5	6-9	10+
16.	Used other illegal drugs?	0	1	2	3-5	6-9	10+
17.	Been involved with a criminal activity (shoplifting, vandalism, etc.)?	0	1	2	3-5	6-9	10+
18.	Not worn your seat belt in the car?	0	1	2	3-5	6-9	10+
19.	Received a failing grade?	0	1	2	3-5	6-9	10+
20.	Been punished for breaking the rules, either at home or at school?	0	1	2	3-5	6-9	10+

Thank You!

On-line Sources of Funding Information

Administration for Children and Families (Social Services Block Grants)

http://www.acf.dhhs.gov/programs/ssbg/index.html

GovCon

http://www.govcon.com

Education and Outreach

http://www.doi.gov/doi_edu.html

Foundation Center

http://www.fdncenter.org/

GrantMatch

http://www.grantmatch.com/grantseekers.html-ssi

GrantSelect

http://www.grantselect.com/

Join Together Online

http://www.jointogether.org/sa/resources/

National Institute of Corrections

http://www.nicic.org/

National Institute on Drug Abuse

http://www.nida.nih.gov/Funding.html

National Institutes of Health

http://www.nih.gov/grants

National Resource Directory of Victim Assistance Funding Opportunities
   http://www.ojp.usdoj.gov/ovc/fund/nrd

Office of Justice Programs
   http://www.ncjrs.org/fedgrant.html

Office of Juvenile Justice and Delinquency Prevention
   http://www.ojjdp.ncjrs.org/grants/grants.html

Safe & Drug Free Schools Program
   http://www.ed.gov/offices/OESE/SDFS/grants.html

Substance Abuse and Mental Health Services Administration
   http://www.samhsa.gov/grants/grants.html

Substance Abuse Funding News
   http://www.cdpublications.com/funding/saf.htm

U.S. Department of Education
   http://www.ed.gov/funding.html

Sample Participant Data Sheet

The name of this program is: _____

1. My age is:

   ☐ 8   ☐ 12   ☐ 16

   ☐ 9   ☐ 13   ☐ 17

   ☐ 10   ☐ 14   ☐ 18+

   ☐ 11   ☐ 15   ☐ Adult (non-student)

2. I am: ☐ Male   ☐ Female

3. I describe myself as:

   ☐ African American

   ☐ American Indian

   ☐ Asian or Pacific Islander

   ☐ Hispanic

   ☐ Caucasian

   ☐ other

4. I will finish this grade this year:

   ☐ 4   ☐ 7   ☐ 10

   ☐ 5   ☐ 8   ☐ 11

   ☐ 6   ☐ 9   ☐ 12

5. I live:

   ☐ on a farm or in the country

   ☐ in a small community

   ☐ in a large community

   ☐ in a city

6. I learned about the program from:
   - ☐ teacher ☐ school counselor
   - ☐ parent ☐ friend
   - ☐ coach ☐ school administrator
   - ☐ other _____

7. Currently my grades are:
   - ☐ Mostly A's
   - ☐ Mostly B's
   - ☐ Mostly C's
   - ☐ Mostly D's
   - ☐ I'm not passing

RESOURCE DD

Data Collection
Timeline Worksheet

Date Due	Task	Responsible Person

A Word on Acronyms

Acronyms are used in this book. Always, the complete title is spelled out in the text. This acronym glossary is provided as a reference so that as you encounter these in your future reading or research, you will be a step ahead.

ATOD	Alcohol, tobacco, and other drugs
CADCA	Community Anti-Drug Coalitions of America
CDC	Centers for Disease Control and Prevention
DEA	Drug Enforcement Administration
DUI	Driving Under the Influence
DWI	Driving While Intoxicated
EDC	Education Development Center
FERPA	Family Educational Rights and Privacy Act
NCADD	National Council on Alcoholism and Drug Dependence
NCJRS	National Criminal Justice Reference Service
NHSDA	National Household Survey on Drug Abuse
NHTSA	National Highway Traffic Safety Administration
NIAAA	National Institute on Alcohol Abuse and Alcoholism
NIDA	National Institute on Drug Abuse
NIH	National Institutes of Health
OESE	Office of Elementary and Secondary Education
OJJDP	Office of Juvenile Justice and Delinquency Prevention
ONDCP	Office of National Drug Control Policy
PPRA	Protection of Pupil Rights Amendment
PRIDE	Parents' Resource Institute for Drug Education
SAMHSA	Substance Abuse and Mental Health Services Administration
SAP	Student Assistance Program
SDFSC	Safe and Drug Free Schools and Communities

Glossary of Terms

Active parent consent   A parent's written consent giving the school permission to include his or her child in any survey, analysis, or evaluation that falls under the PPRA.

Alternate form reliability   Method involving two comparable forms of the same questionnaire—"Form A" and "Form B." The two forms should be as close to identical as possible without actually being the same.

Baseline data   Generally the initial data against which all future data will be measured to determine the direction or magnitude of change.

Comparison data   Data collected from a group with the same general characteristics as the sample population and used for purposes of comparison (e.g., all youth aged 14-15, Hispanic males in Grades 4-5).

Comparison group   A group of the same size and characteristics who receive a separate but largely equivalent program.

Contingency tables   Tables that present numbers and percentages of participants in two or more groups. They are useful when categories are clear-cut, like gender, age, and race.

Control group   A group of the same size and characteristics as those who receive programming, only this group does not participate in programming.

Cost effectiveness   Adding up the actual costs of running your program, divided by the number of students who benefit from your program. Based on the per student cost, determining whether the program is financially efficient and funds are spent concurrently with program goals and objectives.

Criteria referencing   The process of using an independent "criterion" that will measure the same thing as your self-report instrument. For example, let's say a self-report test is designed to select the most promising applicants for an academic program. Then ultimate academic success would be a "criterion" and could be compared to your questionnaire results and used as validation data.

Descriptive analysis   A description, or word picture, of the overall program, goals, variables, and results. It provides general information on how many people participated, program duration, raw numbers and percentages, glitches, and proposed changes.

En-route tests   Measurements taken or tests administered during a program to assess implementation rather than effectiveness.

Error variance   The fluctuations in test performance from one testing session to another.

External validity   Showing a program can produce similar results even with slight variations in the program or program personnel.

Extraneous variable   A variable that is not part of the program design.

Focus group   A structured group interview.

Goal   A statement of direction and intent. *Merriam-Webster's* (1998, p. 499) defines it as "the end toward which effort is directed."

Intervention   An action taken to prevent an action or to maintain or alter a condition. A program is an intervention because it is intended to prevent an increase in risk behaviors or to maintain or reduce current behavior rates.

Measure of central tendency   Any measure that determines the average rate in a given population. Included are the *mean,* or the arithmetic average; the *median,* the central score; and the *mode,* the score that most participants received.

Nonequivalent comparison group   A group of nonrandom assignment with characteristics that may be slightly different from those who receive the program.

Norm   A set standard of development or achievement obtained from the average or median achievement of a large group. Most scores are interpreted by comparison with other scores. The "average" rates of certain behaviors would be the "norms." Raw scores are fairly meaningless without comparative data.

Objective   A statement of action that is more precise and limited than a goal statement. A measurable objective will specify a population or a service, a measurable change, and a deadline for completion.

Objective data   What can be observed and measured. Measurement is key.

Outcome objective   An objective that describes in just one or two sentences exactly how you expect the child, population, or group to look after participating in your program.

Passive parent consent   The school must notify parents that their child will participate in a survey, analysis, or evaluation. The materials that are involved must be made available for parental review. Parents do not have to respond actively unless they do not want their child to participate.

Per student cost The total cost of the program divided by the number of actual students who participated in the program. It is important to use an actual student count, not a duplicated count.

Posttests Tests or measurements made at the end of a program or activity. They are often very similar to pretest instruments to allow for accurate comparison.

Predictive validity Determining levels of risk and protective factors not directly associated with alcohol, tobacco, and other drug use. Determining rates of these indirect behaviors may correlate with deliberate measures of the behaviors you are trying to change, thus "predicting" them.

Pretests Instruments used to collect participant data or measurement before a program or activity.

Prevention Reducing the risk of a specific behavior happening by acting before it begins. A program is preventive if it stops or delays a behavior from starting.

Process objectives Objectives concerned with implementing your program. They are also called implementation objectives.

Qualitative Involving quality or kind. Qualitative information is presented as a narrative or a description.

Quantitative Involving the measurement of precise quantity or amount. Quantitative information is presented numerically.

Quasi-experimental design An experimental design that is not scientifically accurate but that does follow the general principles of scientific method and produces usable results.

Random sample An even mix of academic, race, age, gender, clique, or other demographics.

Raw score All unsummarized and unchanged information that is collected from and about participants.

Reliability Consistency. Predictability. If you use any measuring tool, it should work in a similar way all the time. For example, an odometer should give you the same result for every mile you drive to be considered reliable.

Retest A repeat of the identical test on a second occasion.

Sample The group of people, or the subgroup of the population, you are measuring.

Sampling error   A small or nonrepresentative sample.

Self-report questionnaire   A questionnaire that allows participants to indicate behaviors, attitudes, and knowledge on a particular topic.

Split-half reliability   A single administration of a single questionnaire. Afterward, the items on the questionnaire are separated, or "split," making two comparable halves, such as odd and even.

Standardization   The uniformity of procedures for administering and scoring the instrument.

Subjective information   Nonmeasurable information that includes impressions, judgments, opinions, interpretation of the facts distorted by personal feelings, experiences, or prejudices.

Target population   The group of people, defined by some demographic measure, that has been identified as the recipient of the program.

Time effectiveness   Determining the percentage of staff time dedicated to implementing this program. Is staff time distributed in accordance with program goals and objectives?

Time series analysis   A quasi-experimental method for determining program effectiveness with large populations with infinite variables. It involves collecting measurements of your population for months prior to and subsequent to program implementation. By analyzing the data over time, they may show a change during the period of intervention.

Validity   Whether or not this instrument actually measures what you want it to measure.

Variable   Anything that, when measured, can produce more than two different scores.

References

Allison, K. R., Silverman, G., & Dignam, C. (1990). Effects on students of teacher training in use of a drug education curriculum. *Journal of Drug Education, 20*(1), 31-46.

Bangert-Downs, R. (1988). Effects of school-based substance abuse education: A meta-analysis. *Journal of Drug Education, 18,* 243-264.

Blakely, C., Emshoff, J., & Roitman, D. (1984). Implementing innovative programs in public sector organizations. *Applied Social Psychology Annual: Applications in Organizational Settings, 5,* 87-108.

Botvin, G. J. (1990). Substance abuse prevention: Theory, practice, and effectiveness. In M. Tonry & J. Q. Wilson (Eds.), *Drugs and crime.* Chicago: University of Chicago Press.

Botvin, G. J., Baker, E., Botvin, E. M., Filazzola, A. D., & Millman, R. B. (1989). Prevention of alcohol misuse through the development of personal and social competence: A pilot study. *Journal of Studies on Alcohol,* 550-552.

Brewer, D. D., Hawkins, J. D., Catalano, R. F., & Neckerman, H. J. (1995). Preventing serious, violent, and chronic juvenile offending: A review of evaluations of selected strategies in childhood, adolescence, and the community. In J. C. Howell, B. Krisberg, J. D. Hawkins, & J. J. Wilson (Eds.), *Serious, violent, and chronic juvenile offenders: A sourcebook.* Thousand Oaks, CA: Sage.

Burk, I. (1998). *Guide for school-based drug policy and advisory councils.* Kalamazoo, MI: Balance Group Publishers.

Clark, D. B., Kirisi, L., & Tater, R. E. (1998). Adolescent vs. adult onset and the development of substance use disorders in males. *Drug and Alcohol Dependence, 49,* 115-121.

Connell, D. B., Turner, R. R., & Mason, E. F. (1985, October). Summary of findings of the school health education evaluation: Health promotion effectiveness, implementation, and costs. *Journal of School Health, 55*(8), 316-321.

Drug Strategies. (1998). *Safe schools, safe students: A guide to violence prevention strategies.* Washington, DC: Author.

Drug Strategies. (1999). *Making the grade: A guide to school drug prevention programs—Updated.* Washington, DC: Author.

Dryfoos, J. (1993). *Lessons from evaluation of prevention programs.* Rockville, MD: National Prevention Evaluation Research Collection.

Elias, M. J., & Clabby, J. F. (1984). Integrating social and affective education into public school curriculum and instruction. In C. Maher, R. Illback, & J. Zins (Eds.), *Organizational psychology in the schools: A handbook for professionals*. Springfield, IL: Charles C Thomas.

Goplerup, E. N. (Ed.). (1991). *Preventing adolescent drug use: From theory to practice* (OSAP Prevention Monograph #8). Rockville, MD: U.S. Department of Health and Human Services.

Gottfredson, D. C. (1987). Peer group interventions to reduce the risks of delinquent behavior: A selective review and a new evaluation. *Criminology, 25*, 671-714.

Gottfredson, D. C., Gottfredson, G. D., & Hybl, L. G. (1993). Managing adolescent behavior: A multiyear, multischool study. *American Educational Research Journal, 30*, 179-215.

Gottfredson, D. C., Sealock, M. D., & Koper, C. S. (1996). Delinquency. In R. DiClemente, W. Hansen, & L. Ponton (Eds.), *Handbook of adolescent health risk behavior*. New York: Plenum.

Hansen, W. B., & Graham, J. W. (1991). Preventing alcohol, marijuana, and cigarette use among adolescents: Peer pressure resistance training versus establishing conservative norms. *Preventive Medicine, 20*, 414-430.

Hawkins, J. D., Herrenkohl, T. I., Farrington, D. P., Brewer, D., Catalano, R. F., Harachi, T. W., & Cothern, L. (2000). *Predictors of youth violence* (Juvenile Justice Bulletin #179065). Washington, DC: Office of Juvenile Justice and Delinquency Prevention.

Institute of Medicine (IOM). (1994). *Reducing risks for mental disorders: Frontiers for preventive intervention research*. Washington, DC: National Academy Press.

Klitzner, M. D. (1987). *Report to Congress on the nature and effectiveness of federal, state and local drug prevention/education programs: Part 2. An assessment of the research on school-based prevention programs.* Vienna, VA: Center for Advanced Health Studies.

Lipsey, M. W. (1992). Juvenile delinquency treatment: A meta-analytic inquiry into the variability of effects. In T. D. Cooke, H. Cooper, D. S. Cordray, H. Hartman, L. V. Hedges, R. V. Light, T. A. Louis, & F. Mosteller (Eds.), *Meta-analysis for explanation*. Newbury Park, CA: Sage.

Making the most of your presentation (Youth in Action Bulletin #13). (2000). Washington, DC: U.S. Department of Justice, Office of Justice Programs.

Merriam-Webster's collegiate dictionary (10th ed.). (1998). Springfield, MA: Merriam-Webster.

National household survey on drug abuse. (1998). Rockville, MD: SAMHSA Office of Applied Studies.

Preventing drug use among children and adolescents: A research-based guide (Publication No. 97-4212). (1997). Bethesda, MD: National Institutes of Health, National Institute on Drug Abuse.

Protection of Pupil Rights Amendment (PPRA). Stat: 20 (1978), U.S.C. 1232h; Reg: 34 CFR Part 98.

Resnick, H. (Ed.). (1990). *Youth and drugs: Society's mixed messages* (OSAP Prevention Monograph #6). Rockville, MD: U.S. Department of Health and Human Services.

Rosenbaum, D. P., Flewelling, R. L., Bailey, S. L., Ringwalt, C. L., & Wilkinson, D. L. (1994). Cops in the classroom: A longitudinal evaluation of Drug Abuse Resistance Education (DARE). *Journal of Research in Crime and Delinquency, 31,* 3-31.

Scheirer, M., & Kraut, R. E. (1979). Increasing educational achievement via self-concept change. *Review of Educational Research, 49,* 131-150.

Scheirer, M., & Rezmovic, E. (1982). *Measuring the implementation of innovations.* Annandale, VA: American Research Institute.

Schroeder, D. S., Laflin, M. T., & Weis, D. L. (1993). Is there a relationship between self-esteem and drug use? Methodological and statistical limitations of the research. *Journal of Drug Issues, 23*(4), 645-665.

Sherman, L. W., Gottfredson, D., MacKenzie, D., Eck, J., Reuter, P., & Bushway, S. (1997). *Preventing crime: What works, what doesn't, what's promising.* College Park, MD: U.S. Department of Justice, Office of Justice Programs.

Thomas, S. J. (1999). *Designing surveys that work: A step-by-step guide.* Thousand Oaks, CA: Corwin.

U.S. Department of Education. (1998a). *Nonregulatory guidance for implementing the SDFSCA principles of effectiveness.* Washington, DC: Author.

U.S. Department of Education. (1998b, June 1). Principles of effectiveness (Final version). *Federal Register, 63*(104).

U.S. Department of Education & U.S. Department of Justice. (1999). *1999 annual report on school safety.* Washington, DC: Author.

U.S. Department of Justice, Office of Juvenile Justice and Delinquency Prevention. (2000). *The High/Scope Perry Preschool Project* (Juvenile Justice Bulletin Publication #181725). Washington, DC: Author.

Working with the media (Youth in Action Bulletin #14). (2000). Washington, DC: U.S. Department of Justice, Office of Justice Programs.

Index

CORWIN
PRESS

The Corwin Press logo—a raven striding across an open book—represents the happy union of courage and learning. We area professional-level publisher of books and journals for K-12 educators, and we are committed to creating and providing resources that embody these qualities. Corwin's motto is "Success for All Learners."

SAFETY & SECURITY